An Illustrated History of

CARDIFF DOCKS

Volume 2

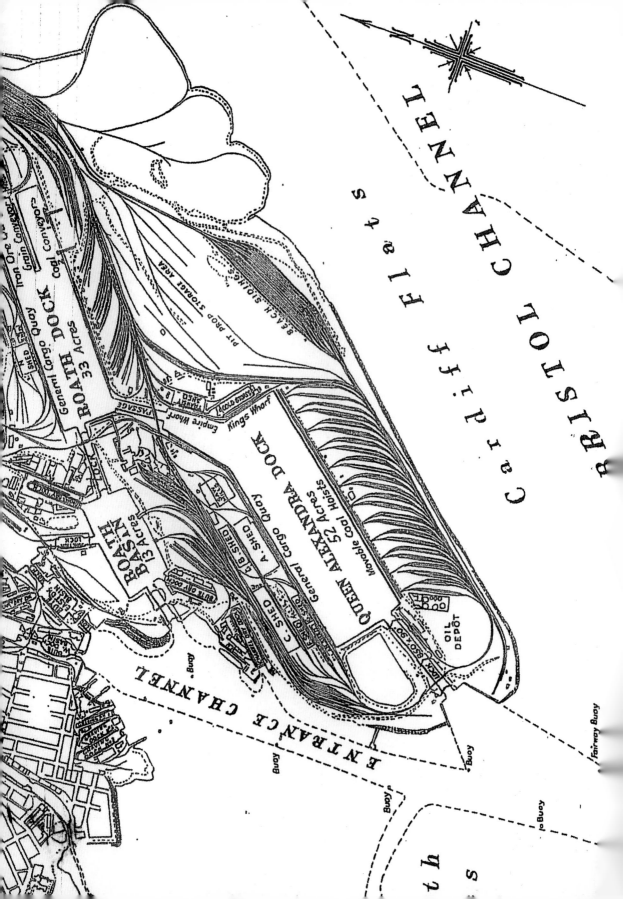

An Illustrated History of

CARDIFF DOCKS

Volume 2:
Queen Alexandra Dock, the Entrance Channel
and Mountstuart Dry Docks

John Hutton

•MARITIME HERITAGE•
from
The NOSTALGIA Collection

This work is dedicated to my stepson, Warrant Officer Brian Edward Nicholls, on his retirement from the 1st Battalion the Welsh Guards after 23 years with the colours, and to his partner and fiancée, Deborah.

First published in 2008

British Library Cataloguing in Publication Data

A catalogue record for this book is available from the British Library.

ISBN 978 1 85794 307 8

Silver Link Publishing Ltd
The Trundle
Ringstead Road
Great Addington
Kettering
Northants NN14 4BW

Tel/Fax: 01536 330588
email: sales@nostalgiacollection.com
Website: www.nostalgiacollection.com

All photographs are from the Associated British Ports collection unless otherwise credited.

Printed and bound in the Czech Republic

A Silver Link book
from
The NOSTALGIA *Collection*

Half title The crest of the Cardiff Railway Company. *Author's collection*

Page 2 A map of Queen Alexandra Dock from a Dock & Harbour Authority booklet of May 1957.

Left Jaffa oranges being unloaded onto British Road Services lorries at Queen Alexandra Dock in 1960. In 1973, after leaving the Army, the author joined BRS at the Pontypool Turnpike Depot, mainly hauling Pilkington glass from their nearby factory. I worked with a good bunch of drivers, who knew their stuff – they literally taught me the ropes.

CONTENTS

SEALS TO BE EXAMINED ON ARRIVAL.

GREAT WESTERN RAILWAY. (2527ᶠ)

SHIPPING GOODS

Date _____192   Train _____

From ABERTHAW (Cement Works)

To CARDIFF DOCKS

Name of
Dock_____

Name of
Ship_____

Consignee _____

Wagon No _____
8 0J0 W 34 11-46.

No. of
Sheets_____

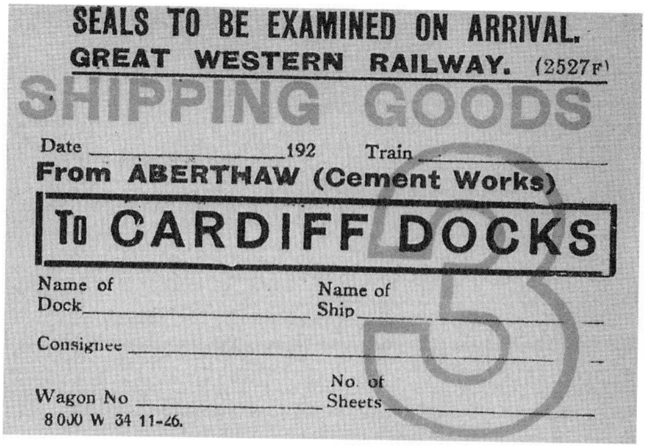

L. D. Bryant collection

A typical post-war scene in Queen Alexandra Dock: a cargo of asphalt is being discharged into railway wagons from the hold of the SS *Painter* on 26 November 1949.

INTRODUCTION

Approval to add another dock to the complex at Cardiff was granted by an Act of Parliament dated 31 July 1894, but considerable difficulties were experienced in raising the necessary capital in view of the high estimated cost arising from the fact that the whole area would have to be reclaimed from the sea. However, by 1898 this had been done and an embankment, 7,700 feet in length, constructed, finally allowing the necessary work to begin on what was then simply called the South Dock.

This dock was opened on 13 July 1907, and the name has changed to the Queen Alexandra Dock, a move influenced by the Royal decision to visit the new facility. On 12 July 1907, the night before the Royal opening, guests and dignitaries were invited to lunch on the Royal Yacht *Victoria and Albert*. The menu, presented on thick card edged in gold, included pea purée soup with croutons, fillet of sole in a white wine sauce, fillet of beef, braised chicken served with a sweet yeast bread, asparagus spears in a butter garlic sauce, creamed rice with strawberries, raspberry compote and roasted woodcock and champagne water-ice.

An article in *The Railway Magazine* of 1908 described the docks thus:

> As a port for the Midlands, Cardiff is unquestionably as convenient as it is near, while by the Great Western Railway's magnificent service of express trains London may be reached by passengers within three

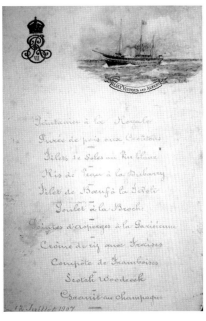

The commemorative medallion struck to celebrate the opening of the Queen Alexandra Dock on 13 July 1907. The obverse bears head-and-shoulder portraits of Their Majesties King Edward VII and Queen Alexandra, while the inscription on the reverse reads: 'To commemorate the visit to the City of Cardiff of the King & Queen & HRH Princess Victoria on the occasion of the opening of the Queen Alexandra Dock 13th July 1907'.

Also shown is the Royal menu from 12 July 1907. *Mrs Lang/Glamorgan Records Office (Ref DIDXKZ5)*

hours. There is, further, an excellent train service to other parts of the country – north, east, and west – so there is no reason why Cardiff should not become a port of call for passenger liners, as Cardiffians shrewdly suggest such vessels would, in addition to other advantages, be able to secure as bunkers the best steam coal the world produces at far less cost than at other ports.

The dock is 2,550 feet long and 800 feet wide, and covers an area of 52 acres.

Top and middle These two photographs show the preparations that had been carried out, and the nervousness of the officials awaiting Their Majesties. The building is believed to have been a temporary wooden construction, located close to the Pierhead Building.

Bottom Their Majesties King Edward VII and Queen Alexandra and HRH Princess Victoria are received by Lord Bute and Sir W. T. Lewis Esq on 13 July 1907. *The Railway Magazine, 1908*

Right A Cardiff Railway Company map of 1904, showing the GWR Bute Docks branch (upper centre), the Rhymney Railway Bute Docks branch alongside it, the short LNWR spur, and the Taff Vale Railway's lines (upper left). Very little detail is as yet shown of 'South Dock', which would become Queen Alexandra Dock. A railway line runs from the storage sidings area (right), skirting the south side of Roath Dock and the roads leading to the coaling staithes. It then crosses the newly formed Communication Passage before travelling along the southern side of the Roath Basin coaling staithes and the Bute Dry Dock, curves around the south-western front of South Dock, then crosses the Entrance Lock via a bridge between the outer and middle lock gates. The map also shows two dry docks parallel to the Entrance Lock. The entire length of the northern side of South Dock is simple described as 'Import wharf and warehouses'. *Author's collection*

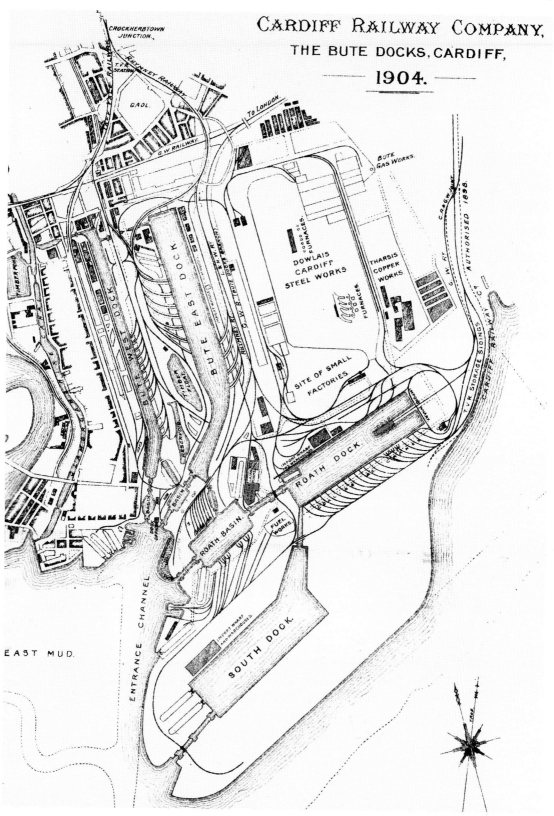

CARDIFF RAILWAY COMPANY,
THE BUTE DOCKS, CARDIFF,
1904.

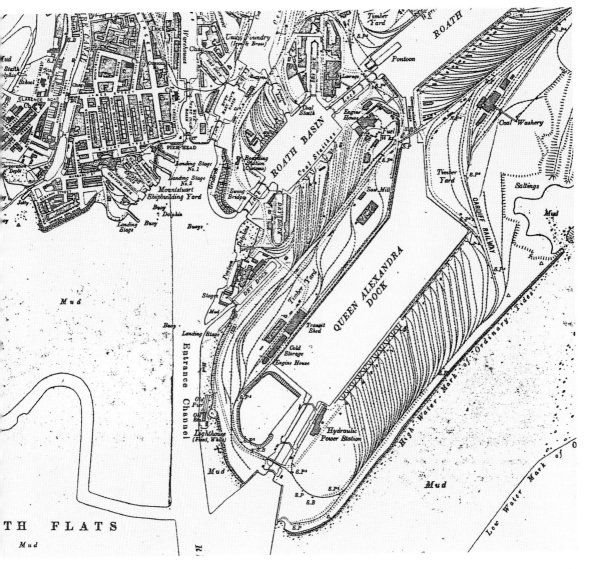

Above An Ordnance Survey map of 1922, showing the layout of Queen Alexandra Dock and the approach to the docks via the Entrance Channel. (See also the map on page 95.) *Crown Copyright*

Above right This aerial photograph was taken on 8 December 1930. On the northern (left) side of Queen Alexandra Dock warehouses have appeared where once stood timber yards and open storage areas. The engine house that stood at the western corner, supplying the power to chill the cold store nearby, can still be seen, as can the cold store itself (later H Shed). To its right, parallel with the dockside cranes, is the Transit Shed (later G Shed), and beyond are the warehouses built on the former timber yard areas between 1922 and 1929. The largest is A Shed, and behind it is the B Shed complex. To the left of B is C Shed, and between it and the waterfront H Shed is F Shed At the top corner of the dock the sawmills are still there, and to their

right is Bell's Wharf and the Communication Passage, on the opposite side of which is Schroeters Wharf (later renamed Empire Wharf) with its five cranes. Behind this wharf, in what would shortly become the pit prop storage area, stands the coal washery building. To the right of Schroeters Wharf is a vessel at berth alongside King's Wharf. On the southern side of the dock are the coaling staithes and cranes, some of which have vessels alongside. Between this dock and Roath Basin a vessel can be seen in the Channel Dry Dock (centre left).

Right Moments later this second photograph was taken. The Communication (or Compass) swing bridge can clearly be seen on the right. To its left, alongside Roath Basin Inner Lock, is the Crown Fuel Plant, and beyond, across the lock, are the cattle lairs. On the left is the Commercial Dry Dock and, close to it, Junction Lock. Bute Dry Dock can also be seen (centre left).

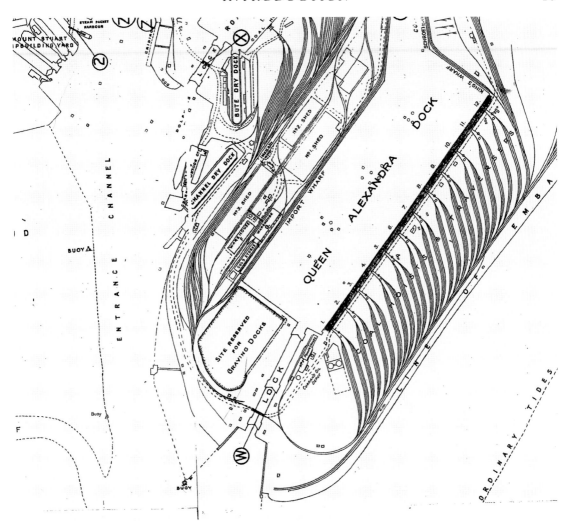

Above left These further aerial views were taken in July 1947, and again show quite clearly the overall layout of Queen Alexandra Dock and Roath Dock and its Basin, as well as the Channel Dry Dock on the Entrance Channel (centre left) and the Bute Dry Dock above it, both of which have ships in them. The Channel Dry Dock, built in 1897 by the Channel Dry Dock & Engineering Company, initially measured 635 feet by 62ft 6in, but was later extended to 635 by 75 feet. The Docks and Harbour booklet of May 1957 says that these dry docks 'maintain a high standard of up-to-date efficiency, including the recent introduction of tank cleaning and gas-freeing plant for the convenience of oil-burning vessels, and oil tankers using this port.' The GKN Steelworks is top left. Top right is the massive area of former salt marshes reclaimed to provide the south-eastern boundary of the docks; today this is outlined by Longships Road. Clearly seen is Empire Wharf, with its transit sheds, and to its right King's Wharf, with its cold store.

Left The second is a view looking south-west. The Entrance Lock and its outer and inner lock gates can be seen in the distance, and to the right of the lock is the timber pond, which was originally to have been dry docks. Fronting the Entrance Channel between the Entrance Lock and the Channel Dry Dock (right centre) can be seen the remains of the low-water pier, with its temporary signal mast just visible. On the northern side of the dock are the aforementioned warehouses, Bell's Wharf and the Communication Passage swing bridge; to the right of the bridge can just be seen the Crown Fuel Works, while nearest the camera is King's Wharf with its cold store and, to the right, Empire Wharf. Out in the Entrance Channel a faithful dredger removes the ever-present mud and silt and keeps the channel passage deep and safe, while beyond her in the distance can be seen the one-time rival docks at Penarth, which in all but name belonged to the Taff Vale Railway.

Above An Ordnance Survey map of 1946, showing the Queen Alexandra Dock and the Entrance Channel. *Crown Copyright*

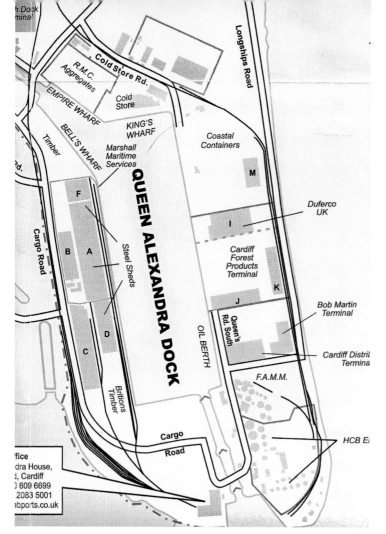

Queen Alexandra Dock today.

fice
dra House,
1, Cardiff
) 609 6699
2083 5001
abports.co.uk

ABP

CARDIFF – VESSELS DUE
21ˢᵗ APRIL 2006
HIGH WATER: 1257

VESSELS IN PORT

LOCATION	VESSEL	TO/FROM	CARGO	TONNES	D/L	AGENTS
Roath Dock	STS Cymru	UK	~	~	~	Bay Shipping
Coastal	Coastal Isle	Dublin	Containers	~	D/L	Coastal Containers
No 1 Berth	Alderbaron	Ayr	Steel	~	D	Cardiff Stevedores
Texaco	Alsterstern	Pembroke Dock	Tanker	~	D	OBC Shipping
Hanson	Arco Dart	Channel Banks	Sand	~	D	Hanson

VESSEL ARRIVALS PENDING

DUE DATE	VESSEL	TO/FROM	CARGO	TONNES	D/L	AGENTS
23 April	Fehn Sun	Milazzo	Steel Beams	2800T	D	Graypen
25 April	Bro Gratitude	Plymouth	Tanker	~	D	OBC Shipping
26 April	Mount Troodos	Rosyth	Scrap	~	L	Bay Shipping
26 April	Bremer Victoria	Norrsundej	Timber	2890cbn	D	C M Willie
26 April	Coral Sea	Turkey	Cat Litter	~	D	Harvest Shipping
27 April	Arklow Sand	Santander	Steel	2920	D	C M Willie
28 April	BNS Bellis	~	Belgian Warship	~	~	TBN
28 April	BNS Stern	~	Belgian Warship	~	~	TBN
30 April	Minitank One	Lavera	Tanker	~	D	Graypen
19 May	HMS Atherstone	~	Royal Navy	~	~	HMS Cambria
19 May	HMS Middleton	~	Royal Navy	~	~	HMS Cambria
19 May	HMS Walney	~	Royal Navy	~	~	HMS Cambria

The dock is still busy with imports exports. This 'Vessels due' list is dated 21 April 2006.

1. THE QUEEN ALEXANDRA DOCK

The Entrance Lock

The Entrance Lock is 850 feet long and 90 feet wide, with a high-water depth of 42ft 2in at spring tide, and 32ft 7in on a neap tide. When opened in 1907 it consisted of three lock gates – outer, middle and inner – with a single-track railway line crossing the lock between the outer and middle gates. The deepening of this entrance lock now enables vessels of 30,000grt to use the dock and the adjoining Roath Dock. Queen Alexandra Dock itself has an average water depth of 37 feet, increasing to 39ft 3in at high water on an ordinary spring tide, and on a neap tide as low as 29ft 9in.

The Ordnance Survey map of 1922 (page 10) shows a hydraulic power station next to the inner gate of the Entrance Lock. Hydraulic power was maintained at a pressure of 800psi over the whole dock system using eight power houses (in 1920); some 23 engines, all working in harmony, maintained the pressure needed to work the coaling cranes, tips and the numerous general cargo cranes, lifts varying from 35cwt to 70 tons. In Queen Alexandra Dock in 1920 there were eight electric and ten steam cranes, in addition to the numerous hydraulic cranes. On the 1946 map (page 13) the hydraulic power station has become the No 1 Power House.

In May 1957 work was in progress to update this equipment, as the Docks & Harbour Authority booklet states:

Both the Mechanical and Electrical Engineers Department and the Civil Engineers Department have been concerned in the major scheme for the electrification of the No 1 Power Station, Queen Alexandra Dock, which necessitated the installation of new electric impounding hydraulic and house drainage pumps. A good deal of reconstruction work has been necessary to

railway bridges, swing bridges, etc, as a result of the long war period, when no major works could be undertaken, and the Civil Engineers Department have also renewed the dock gates at the Queen Alexandra Dock Outer Lock.

In the western corner of the dock, north-west of the Entrance Lock, was a large reservoir, or Timber Pond, large enough to match the entire length of the nearby lock. On the OS map of 1946 (page 13) this area is marked as 'site reserved for graving docks', (as had originally been intended back in 1904). However, by the 1980s the area had been abandoned and looked rather desolate, covered by weeds. By 2007 this area of waterfront had become part of Britton's Timber Ltd, subsequently occupied by Messrs F. W. Morgan, an old-established Cardiff firm, as its new timber berth. Nearby a new road, Locks Road, joins Cargo Road. In 2003 the railway line that for many years had skirted this proposed dry docks area was severed and no longer crossed over the new roller bridge (which had replaced the former 1904 swing bridge in 1995). This single-track line crossed the Entrance Lock to connect with the storage sidings, and Cardiff Railway locomotives handled the movement of wagons from the sidings into the docks complex itself.

South of the Entrance lock, which was once waste ground, was the site of Curran's Oil Depot by 1946/47. This new traffic brought yet bigger ships. In the spring of 1963 *Ship Ahoy* magazine reported that the largest ship ever to dock at Cardiff, the tanker *Continental I* (17,845gt), carrying a 7,000-ton part cargo of petroleum for the Jet company's installation, had arrived on 22 January. Owned by World Wide Transport Inc of New York, the ship was 625 feet long by 84ft 7in wide – the Entrance Lock is just 90 feet wide.

By 1982 this area was marked on maps as an Oil

Berth, and Texaco Ltd was alongside Curran's depot. From 2003 until 2007 this area was the site for FAMM and HCB Energy, a firm that operated a multi-purpose fuel oil, chemical and distillate storage facility for customers such as Dow Chemicals and Arkema, as well as the storing of molasses for SVG Intermol Ltd. Dow Chemicals closed in 2006, Arkema now import their caustic soda, and SVG Intermol Ltd have ceased storing

molasses since 2006. Today Inver Energy UK Ltd occupies these sites alongside the Entrance Lock outer gates, and on Cargo Road is the new Associated British Ports office block.

In 1987 the decision was made to use the Queen Alexandra Dock Entrance Lock for all vessels using both that dock and Roath Dock, which would be reached via the Communication Passage.

Above This is the Entrance Lock for the new 'South Dock' under construction as seen from the sea gates on 4 August 1905. One lock wall has been completed, and work is proceeding on the middle lock gate sill. Steam-operated derrick cranes can be seen on both sides of the lock.

Left This view of the inner gate sill and lock floor was also taken on 4 August 1905. It shows the sill under construction and sluice culvert openings in the wall behind; the lock floor has not yet been formed.

Right The new Entrance Lock in about 1907.

Below right The new Queen Alexandra Dock is seen from the inner lock gates in about 1908. This was a very well-designed dock, providing direct access and large enough to handle the volume of shipping that would use it over the ensuing years.

Below The Entrance Lock is seen here circa 1946. In the foreground is the sea wall with the sluice and impounding culvert entrances exposed. The lock is open to the channel and the swing bridge gives access to road and rail traffic. To the left of the bridge is the area of water that was originally to have been three graving docks, while to the right are some small buildings used by the lock gate operators and maintenance staff. At the far end of the lock, to the right of the inner gate, is the tall chimney of the Impounding (also known as Hydraulic) Pump House. Behind it, and attached to the chimney, is the Steam Generating Boiler House, beside which is a line of railway wagons, delivering coal for the boilers. The square tower alongside housed the hydraulic accumulator, which helped to maintain a constant pressure supply to the machinery around the dock. Beyond

this complex can be seen the coaling hoists on the southern side of the dock. At the top of the dock is the cold store on King's Wharf, and to the left Schroeters (Empire) Wharf and

the Communication Passage, giving access into Roath Dock. By 1946 the area to the right of the road by the Pump House would soon house the tanks of the Curran Oil Company.

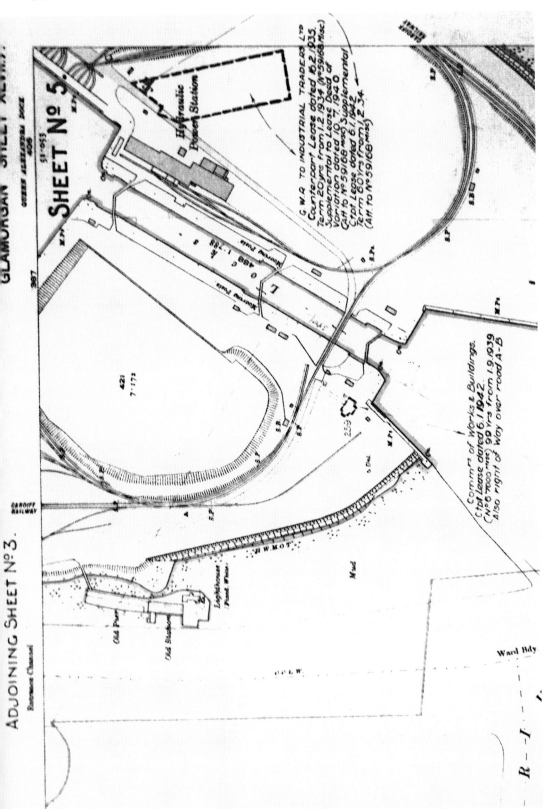

This 1920 map of the Entrance Lock area shows the various agreements, leases and conditions, etc, made by the Great Western Railway in the 1930s to tenants such as Industrial Traders Ltd and the Commissioners of Works and Buildings.

Above   HMS *Neptune* enters the Entrance Lock accompanied by the steam tug *The Earl* on 13 May 1935.

Left Repairs are being undertaken to the Entrance Lock floor and lock gate sill in May 1937. The floor and sill were regularly inspected by divers to detect any deterioration. In this case the lock has been emptied, revealing the sluice culvert apertures in the wall behind the hand crane; these culverts allowed the water levels in the lock to be adjusted.

Left A close-up of the floor of the emptied Entrance Lock, showing the repairs being undertaken to return the lock to service as quickly as possible.

Above M/V *Cumberland* enters the Entrance Lock in the tow of an unidentified steam tug in June 1949. The swing bridge is in the open position, while on the left the waste ground is being prepared for new occupancy.

Below Some years later the Regent oil tank facility has arrived. The 1904-vintage swing bridge is seen here in its closed position, ie open for road traffic use.

Above Mine-layer and flagship of the Home Fleet HMS *Apollo*, C167, visits Queen Alexandra Dock in the Coronation year of 1953. Behind her is the tall chimney of the dock Impounding Station, and in the far background is the cold store at King's Wharf. On the right the wilderness of former waste ground has given way to the newly established Curran Oils complex. Note the white painted line on the lock's coping stones, a wartime blackout safety measure.

Right Once again, in 1967, the lock is dry. It was necessary to completely empty the Entrance Lock as water pressure under the lock floor was causing a section of the floor to deteriorate, so a series of ground anchors were installed to strengthen and stabilise the area. On 20 July an operation is in progress to remove the lock inverts.

Right While the work was taking place on the same day, this foundation stone was uncovered and photographed.

Above left HMS *Warspite* enters Queen Alexandra Dock's Entrance Lock from the Entrance Channel in 1972, with her periscope raised, while at the base of the very crowded conning tower is the ship's bell. At the front of this nuclear-powered submarine can be seen her forward hydroplanes. In line with the conning tower are the lock's middle gates, open and fitting snugly in their wall recesses. Beyond, in front of the outer gate, are the tugs *Bowgarth* and *Danegarth*.

Left Entering the lock in January 1974 is the MV *Drakenstein*, providing another good view of the swing bridge. In the distance, high up on Penarth Heights, the silhouette of the Church of St Augustine stands out. Mr Bill Osborn, who worked as a foreman in the Mountstuart and Channel dry docks for a total of 16 years, told me a story about the bells of this church. One of his fellow workers was a member of the church, and the congregation wanted to hear the bells peal out for Christmas, some 50 years ago. However, the bells were broken, and Bill was asked if he could repair them, which he did. Now, even after so many years, every time he sees the church the memories come flooding back.

Above Photographed on 23 April 2006, looking from Longships Road towards the new Associated British Ports offices on Cargo Road, is the roller (or retractable) bridge, with flashing lights to warn road traffic. Instead of swinging it slowly rolls towards the office side of this lock until no longer an obstruction to seaborne traffic. This bridge replaced the original 1904 one in 1995. *Author*

Right The new ABP plaque and the Cardiff Railway Co plaque of 1904 were photographed on 22 October 2003. The latter bears the inscription 'Superstructure made and erected by Andrew Handyside & Co Limited, Derby. Hydraulic machinery made and erected by Sir W. G. Armstrong, Whitworth & Co Ltd, Newcastle-on-Tyne. *Author*

North side:
the general cargo quay

After passing through the Queen Alexandra Dock inner lock caisson gates, we enter the dock itself. Moving along the north (strictly north-western) side, the 1920s map shows the former Import Wharf with its Cold Store. By 1913 Cardiff was the third most important port in Great Britain for the importation of frozen meat, being excelled only by London and Liverpool. In 1914 a new brick-built cold store was opened at this extreme western end of the dock, with a quayside frontage of 300 feet (today this area is still known as the No 1 Berth). The store had one receiving floor, for the storage of sundry goods, and three refrigerated floors for frozen meat, each containing three chambers measuring 300 feet by 50 feet wide, giving a storage capacity of 300,000 cubic feet. In 1938 this cold store was stripped of its refrigerating plant and was from then onwards used as a warehouse for general cargoes, known as H Shed.

A further warehouse behind the former cold store was known as F Shed, and another beside H Shed was known as G Shed; G and H Sheds were demolished in December 1971. A new D Shed, of steel construction, was built in 1972 and covered the area of the former F, G and H Sheds.

The 1940s OS maps shows three large new warehouses. One, No 3 shed, is situated behind F Shed, with No 2 behind No 1, the latter located on the wharf front. No 3 shed, of brick construction, was used for grain and general cargo storage, and measuring 722 feet by 144 feet wide; it is now known as C shed. No 1 shed was another of brick construction, with one floor measuring 602 feet by 203 feet wide and used not only for grain but also for the storage of general cargo; this is now A Shed. No 2 Shed was also of brick, and was used for grain and general cargo storage; it measures 441 feet by 123 feet and is now called B Shed. These sheds were erected by the Ministry of Shipping to deal with any emergencies that might arise during the war years; after the war they were purchased by the Dock Authority, and by 1957 had been renamed A (No 1), B (No 2) and C (No 3) Sheds.

After passing the A Shed/No 1 Shed complex, the remainder of this side of the dock was home to a massive timber yard, with a timber shed and its sawmill located at the north-west corner; this

belonged to Bill Price, a well-known timber merchant. The building of Nos 1 and 2 Sheds left the sawmills, timber shed and timber yard much reduced in size. In 1980 the new steel D and brick A Sheds were joined by a new steel F Shed, replacing the old sawmill complex. In front of this F Shed, at the dockside, is Marshall Maritime Services.

The nearby wharf is known as Bell's Wharf, after the firm of C. P. Bell & Co, pit prop importers. Today this wharf is part of the Cardiff Forest Products group, operated by Cardiff Stevedoring Ltd, which handles the timber products that are supplied by Messrs C. M. Willie Shipping Company, established in Cardiff in 1929 as Celtic Lines. It almost seems that the dock is reverting to its original purpose, the handling timber and steel – perhaps in the not so distant future we may yet see coal here again!

At Bell's Wharf the top corner of Queen Alexandra Dock takes on a funnel-like shape. This is the start of Communication Passage, leading towards the Communication Bridge.

Four new 2-ton hydraulic derricking jib-cranes have been brought into use at the new Queen Alexandra Dock of the Cardiff Railway at Cardiff. The cranes are each capable of lifting, derricking, and turning, all at the same time, with a full load of 2 tons on, and the general design of the cranes and the various parts are so constructed as to be easily accessible for examination at any time.

*   *   *

The estimate of capital expenditure on the Cardiff Railway for the current half-year is £50,000. During the first half of 1908 it amounted to £239,235. Of this sum, £48,129 referred to the construction and equipment of the Queen Alexandra Dock.

Above Extract from *The Railway Magazine*, November 1908.

Below Warehouses along Queen Alexandra Dock, believed to be in the south-western corner, which later became the site for the cold store. *The Railway Magazine, July 1908*

Above SS *City of Paris* (9,700 tons) loading rails at Queen Alexandra Dock in about 1922.

Below Raw sugar is being discharged from the SS *Author*, circa 1935. Amongst all the noise and activity horse-drawn carts wind their way between rows of waiting railway vans. In the foreground transhipping between an open wagon and a covered van is taking place. GWR *Ports booklet of 1937*

H Shed

Above French pit wood is being discharged direct from the vessel SS *China* to waiting railway wagons on 7 April 1946, with H Shed on the left. They are a mixed rake of eight- and seven-plank open types, some of which are of former private-owner vintage, the others GWR. The number '1' appears on the leg of this Stothert & Pitt crane, possibly one of a batch ordered in 1932. At this time, soon after the end of the Second World War, many vessels still carried their wartime

equipment, as seen here in the form of quick-release life rafts, essential for saving seamen helpless in the water, especially after an air attack or during the aftermath of a torpedo strike on the hull, which could send a vessel to the bottom within minutes.

Below The SS *Fort Jasper* is also discharging pit props in about 1946. These Canadian-built 'Fort'-type vessels were smaller in size than the United States-built 'Liberty' ships, and were of split-superstructure design.

On 1 August 1946 the SS *Seaside* is discharging a cargo-hold full of Canadian flour, all 8,800 tons of it, to H Shed and to road and rail vehicles, the latter consisting of an LMS van (nearest the camera) then two GWR Fruit Vans.

Down in the hold of the SS *Seaside* on the same day the bags of flour are being lifted out of the hold by the use of strops, rather than pallets, mainly due to the lack of space, but also because this bag cargo is destined for road and rail transport and, properly landed, the strops could be withdrawn without the cargo spilling, thus preventing double handling, ie manhandling the sacks onto pallets then manhandling them off again. Normally the tallyman or checker would be shore-based, but in this photograph he can be seen on the weather deck in shirt sleeves.

Above The SS *Inishowen Head* is discharging general cargo, including foodstuffs from the USA, beside H Shed in August 1946. The electric crane operator and the dockers are skilfully making use of trestles placed outside the railway van doorways to balance the goods for transfer into the vans. These LMS vans are vacuum-brake-fitted for use with main-line passenger traffic or on a fast freight train.

Below This view shows the *Empire Spartan* discharging her cargo of crushed bones at the No 1 berth alongside H Shed some time in August 1948. Once unloaded into the open railway wagons, the tarpaulin sheets are pulled into place, protecting the cargo from inclement weather; the sheets can be seen rolled up in a line between the wagons and the crane tracks.

Right In this busy scene in 1952 timber is being unloaded into a varied mixture of railway wagons below – no wonder the photographer is standing on one of the stages protruding from H Shed!

Below This view of the western corner of Queen Alexandra Dock is looking in the opposite direction in February 1956. Three electrically operated, portal, level luffing cranes by Stothert & Pitt Ltd hold centre stage: nearest the camera No 3 has a 15-ton lift, while Nos 2 and 1 are probably of 6-ton lifting capacity. The former GWR van nearest the camera has a curved wooden roof, while the third van is of LMS design. The road vehicles parked beneath the cranes are, from front to rear, two AEC Mammoth Majors Mk 3, then a Foden, while between these and the railway vans is a Foden DG, all belonging to the nationalised British Road Services. Each carries its depot initials together with a fleet number; the leading AEC, registration number GBO 131, carries BRS number 2G522 next to the 'lion and wheel' symbol on the cab door. A tarpaulin is in position on top of his load, ready to cover it; these were heavy and dirty when dry, and a lot more so when wet. Once the load was roped and sheeted, with his delivery notes in hand and log book updated the driver and perhaps his mate (if he was given one) would be ready for the road.

Driving a load as heavy as this gave you strong biceps – there was no power-assisted steering then – and you also had to double de-clutch, because most of these British-made vehicles (right up to the late 1970s) were fitted with 'crash' gearboxes. This meant that you had to be professional in your driving, have a knowledge of the road, and have skill in the handling and security of your load. At the berth is the *Oorderhaven*, port of registration Groningen, discharging her cargo of potash.

Top In front of H Shed in about 1960 is a line of road vehicles. On the right, with a trailer behind, probably already loaded up, is a British Road Services Maudsley Mogul, with a 'Waste paper is still needed' advert, while on the left is an ERF CI 5, also with a trailer attached and awaiting its turn for its load of tea chests. The 'Iron Mink' railway vans in the left foreground are of former GWR origin.

Middle and bottom The Stothert & Pitt cranes outside H Shed are discharging a cargo of 2,500 tons of cocoa beans from the MV *Dumbaia* (1960, 6,558gt) of the Henderson Line in June 1960. This was the first cargo of its kind to be handled at the port, and was discharged into the warehouse where it was held until required by the Cadbury chocolate company. On the right of the lower view are some internal-user wagons laden with sawn timber planking. The shunting tractor seen in the centre was used when a locomotive, or ground capstan, was not available to position railway vehicles.

Above In another scene outside H Shed, timber is being unloaded onto road and rail vehicles in about 1966. On the right is a Bristol HA6, behind which is a Ford Thames Trader; on the left is an AEC Mercury, and behind is another Bristol HA6 followed by another Ford Thames Trader, all belonging to British Road Services. *Ship Ahoy* reported that the number of timber ships in Cardiff on 27 July 1964 had caused delays in the port, with six ships unloading and two waiting for berths, while another three arrived before the end of the month. The total landed during this spate of activity was more than 23,700 tons.

Below Inside H Shed on 22 January 1957 a variety of goods have been unloaded and are now stored here – cardboard boxes, large sacks and wooden boxes.

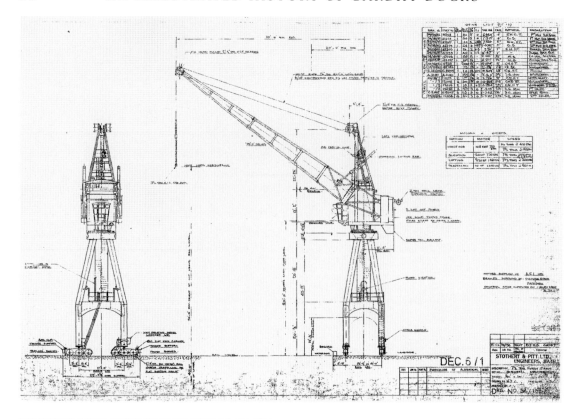

Above Dimensioned drawings of a Stothert & Pitt Ltd DD2-type 7½-ton cargo crane.

Left Under construction in about 1966, these DD2 cranes will soon be operating; one has had its jib attached, while the jib of the other can be seen resting on the quayside alongside the 15-ton cranes, which are being used in the assembly work, as also is the roof of H Shed. A further six of these cranes were purchased and in place by 1967 and they were numbered 8 to 15. Near No 1 berth, we have a good view of the Cardiff tug *Butegarth* (1966, 161gt), owned by R. & J. H. Rea Ltd, which suggests that it may well be in attendance to the floating crane. On the rear deck of the tug can be seen a series of raised transverse steel hoops; these are known as towbeams, or strongbacks, and prevent the towline from snagging, fouling or damaging the tug's afterdeck fittings.

Above This rear view of H Shed in January 1971 shows a mass of sports cars all awaiting export. Nearest the camera are a collection of MGB GTs (introduced in 1965), of coupé design; among them are quite a lot of the MG Roadsters (introduced in 1962), a soft-top convertible sports car. Beneath the middle window of the smaller building are a collection of Hillman Avengers. By the end of the year this building had gone.

Right The date is 17 February 1977, and container traffic has arrived. On the right is a Ford Transit van, while in the centre is a Austin Maxi car. In the background several DD2 cranes are in use, and on the left the new docks insignia can be seen above the sliding doors of the new D Shed. With its blue paint on a steel-covered girder frame, this container storage area would become a timber storage area some ten years later. Note to the left of the container trailer the official wooden box – this is a 'tally hut' supplied by the British Transport Docks Board as protection against the cold for its 'tallymen'. A wooden plinth seat was located inside, and you could guarantee that it would not be long before a burning brazier, usually an empty oil-drum, was stationed by the open side to help ward off the cold wind.

Above This is the lower end of the northern side of Queen Alexandra Dock on 23 April 2006. Today this area is occupied by Messrs F. W. Morgan Ltd, and is seen here from the former (now severed) rail access gate into the timber yard. In the left background is the brick-built C Shed, with D Shed, used for steel storage, on the right. *Author*

G Shed

Below This view shows the SS *Mosnes* discharging her cargo of bagged grain in May 1950. G Shed is on the extreme right, with the taller H Shed beyond. On the left (on the 'water road') is a former GWR 10-ton van, No 02745, wearing the painted cross (internal use only) symbol and a tin roof bolted into place. Behind it is a ventilated van, No W79070, then another van, No M506029; on the right are vans fitted with vacuum brakes.

Right This 'pigeon's-eye' view shows the SS *Caledonia* alongside G Shed discharging crushed bones from Karachi in August 1951. The cargo is going direct into sheeted open wagons. From left to right, the railway lines are the stage road (next to the loading platform or staging), No 1 road, No 2 road, and finally the water road (alongside the waterfront and running under the cranes' legs). In the distance a vessel is at berth at Bell's Wharf.

Below This is the SS *Welsh Prince* taking on board a cargo of steel tubes for North America in August 1952. On the right are some 20-ton tube-carrying wagons – that nearest the camera is No M492071 – while over on the left are some bolster wagons, also loaded with steel tubes waiting to be unloaded. Looking down, cigarette in mouth, the driver of the nearest crane, his window open, carefully controls his load as it swings over towards this ship's hold.

Left An interior view of G Shed on 22 January 1957 shows cargoes unloaded from various vessels – paper from Finland, barrels of ferro-manganese (used in the making of alloy steels), and strips of steel en route for the GKN works.

Between G and A Sheds

Below We are now in the space between G Shed and A Shed, on the north side of Queen Alexandra Dock. It is January 1946 and Britain is in dire need of houses for people made homeless by German bombers during the Second World War. Here we see prefabricated houses from Sweden, arriving on the SS *Rolf*, being discharged into internal user wagons.

These are all four-plank open wagons: the two on the left are of 5 tons 2 cwt tare weight, while that on the right is of 5-8 tare. They are of GWR origin, and the right-hand one bears the words 'For use at Cardiff Docks only' and 'Not to run more than 3 miles on the main lines'. Temporary these houses may have been intended to be, but some prefabricated housing estates lasted right up to the beginning of this century – more than 54 years.

Right The post-war years were a period of rebuilding, and housing estates were growing in places that, before the war, had been green fields. Such was the rate of construction that home-made supplies had to be supplemented from abroad, and this October 1946 view shows bricks from Belgium being double-handled from the hold of the SS *Drakedene*; this involved them being manhandled individually onto the nearby pallet by this group of men, a slow and labour-wasting effort, while on shore another group would restack them. On close inspection these are either poor-quality seconds, or even re-used second-hand bricks.

Below Also in about 1946 sawn planks of wood are being unloaded into open railway wagons. In the left distance can be seen the cold store at King's Wharf, while on the right, over the water, a vessel is taking on coal. The Dock & Harbour Authority booklet of May 1957 stressed the importance of the timber trade: 'The importation of timber has always been a feature of the trade of Cardiff Docks, and this is easily understood in view of the large quantities of pit wood and mining timber regularly required for use in the South Wales coalfields, apart from the requirements of building and wood-working industries in South Wales and the Midlands. Generally speaking pit wood, mainly from Canada, Newfoundland, Scandinavia, France, Spain, Portugal and Finland, is imported for direct despatch to the various local collieries, but large stocks of pit props from similar sources are regularly held at these docks, for which purpose excellent stacking grounds are available. Other classes of timber, both hard and soft, are dealt with by a number of large importing firms who measure, classify, store and subsequently despatch according to specification the numerous kinds of wood held in stock at their establishments on the Docks Estate. Many different varieties of timber are imported, including battens and boards from Russia, Scandinavia, the Baltic and Canada, logs, baulks and sawn wood from the USA and Canada, oak from America, Poland and Yugoslavia, and various other woods from Canada, Burma, Central Europe, etc. Good storage ground is available for the imported wood, and water storage is provided for log and baulk timber, the timber pond being connected to the main dock system by canal.'

Above There's plenty of work for the crane driver here, shipping wire rod into the hold of the SS *Empire Freetown* during May 1946, another vessel still carrying its quick-release life rafts. It was built during the Second World War on behalf of the Ministry of Shipping, hence the prefix 'Empire'. By 1997 only 33 of these vessels, from more than 1,000 built, remained in service.

Below SS *Samdak* is discharging government stores from Italy circa 1946, including returning HM Forces equipment, lorries and guns. The vehicle on the right is a Morris Commercial 4 x 4 truck carrying an anti-aircraft predictor, intended to work with similar vehicles mounting Bofors anti-aircraft guns, while over on the left is a line-up of 5.5-inch anti-tank guns.

These motor cars have been unloaded from the SS *Empire Moufliar* at Queen Alexandra Dock in November 1945; the one on the left is an American-built Buick, destined for the Chinese Ambassador.

In September 1946 we see the shipment of a motor cavalcade. A Humber Snipe is being lowered into the hold of the small coaster *Brockley Combe*, possibly heading to Northern Ireland, before going overseas – its destination is not recorded. The Army registration number on the bonnet, M239459, indicates that this is Monty's car, the one he rode in during the victory parade through the port of Tripoli after its capture by the 8th Army on 23 January 1943. The hood is folded back, revealing two rifle securing clips, and at the rear are two British-made petrol cans holding 5 gallons each, which were renowned for leaking seams and the notorious blow-back of air-trapped fuel when being emptied; it was little wonder the 8th Army's 'Desert Rats' turned them into cooking ovens, and whenever possible used the better-quality German Army 'Jerry cans' instead!

Another car from the motor cavalcade tour is carefully hoisted aboard ship. The group of men at the bottom of this photograph are obviously connected with the cavalcade – the gentleman on the right, wearing the trench coat, has an uncanny resemblance to Viscount Montgomery of Alamein! Perhaps just a coincidence, but it was in September 1946 that Montgomery relinquished his post as Commander in Chief of the British Army based in France and Germany.

Left Ancient and historical seemed to be the theme for the motor cavalcade. Here the single vehicle sling is being put to good use as the crane driver gently lowers the vehicle into the ship's hold. The majority of quayside cranes at use in Cardiff Docks at this time, September 1946, were from the Bath firm of Stothert & Pitt, and were all electrically operated level luffing cranes, ie the jib is hinged at its lower end and the load remains at the same height when luffing in or out. Their lift capacity was either 3 or 6 tons, at a radius (or outreach) of 55 feet, and they were designed to handle general cargoes of all kinds.

Below The *Brockley Combe* carried more than one type of cargo, and seen here is a Bedford removals van en route home to Belfast. This type of van body, with a box placed over the driver's cab, is known as a 'Luton', and originated when the hat manufacturers of Luton needed a big spacious body in which to pack boxes of straw hats, a product that at one time made the town of Luton famous. Officially, such removal vans were known as 'pantechnicons'.

Right Taken in October 1946, at first glance this looks like small boats passing between two vessels. However, all is not what it seems, for this is an American-built Landing Ship Dock (LSD) delivered under the wartime 'lease lend' arrangement and returned after the war. They were built in batches of one or two at a time, and each batch differed in design from the following one. Later they formed the prototype for improved designs with the Royal Navy's HMS *Fearless* (L10) and HMS *Intrepid* (L11).

Below The label on the back of this photograph reads 'Naval small craft carrier taking in craft at Queen's Dock, Cardiff, 25/10/46'. This is the same vessel, but now the water has been pumped out and the small craft are docked safely inside the LSD. Although American-built, the vessel is manned by a British crew and the small craft are decommissioned Motor Torpedo Boats (MTBs). The LCD's superstructure has been painted peacetime white – gone is the battleship grey paint of the wartime years.

Left These AEC road vehicles belong to the Anglo-Iranian Oil Company, and are awaiting their turn to be loaded into the hold of the SS *Ampleforth* in December 1946. Seen in the left background is G Shed, which at this time was used by HM Customs & Excise. An elevated passageway connects this building with C Shed, on the right, while in the background is the tall H Shed. Some 25 years later, in December 1971, G and H Sheds were demolished.

Below Snow-covered or wet ground makes any industrial area a dangerous place, slippery and cold, and 26 February 1947 was one of the coldest. However, it has not stopped the work, and steel pipes are being loaded aboard the SS *Kohistan* as safely as possible. In the background can be seen the A Shed complex.

Right There's better weather in July 1948, and another normal day's work for this 15-ton crane, as it supports a single-decker bus on its journey to the waiting coastal vessel, en route for Ireland. A single vehicle sling is being used, with protective 'palliasse' bags covering the wheel and mudguard areas. The insignia on the side of this bus reads 'Great Northern Railway Ireland', and the coachwork is by Park Royal. The crane driver looks on from his elevated cab.

John O'Brien was a crane-driver at Cardiff for 15 years, and he provides an insight into what was must have been a unique experience: 'Crane-driving may seem to many people to be a lonely job, but this is not so, for the crane driver is the one person who is at the heart of an operation at all times, and all that is to be done actually depends on the crane. You soon get over the fact that you are high above, then you appreciate the whole scene, for you have the overview. There are actually very few controls: on one side is the luff, which controls the neck of the crane, while on the other side the controls turn the crane left or right, and control the lifting cable as it goes up or down. Also, there is a small foot-brake, rarely used, but it helps to control the crane in light winds. The feeling you get is like when you have driven a car on a long journey, and when you arrive you don't remember the last ten miles – that is when you know you can drive a crane, when your movements are automatic and smoothly done. A good crane driver is worth his weight in gold to those men below him, the ganger and his crew, especially when they are working on piecework rates of pay.'

Below The MV *Cumberland* discharges frozen meat to road and rail vehicles in June 1949. The containers seen on the nearest road vehicle (an AEC), with its trailer alongside, belong to the Hay's Wharf Cartage Company, and are similar in principle to the container at the rear of the rake of covered open wagons on the right, a British Railways 'Insul-Meat' container, No 1030, carried on wagon No M474784.

Above A close-up view of the unloading of the frozen meat from the MV *Cumberland*. Temporary boards, supported on wooden trestles, bring the door levels of both rail and road vehicles in line. Once the netting has been swung near to either doorway, it will require little effort to remove these carcases of frozen lamb and place them inside, under the watchful eye of the 'tallyman' with his book.

Below Another part of the cargo carried by the *Cumberland* was cheese, seen here being unloaded into railway wagons with the use of a bale sling. The ship belonged to the Federal Steam Navigation Company Ltd, of London, and travelled to and from the United Kingdom via America, Australia and New Zealand.

Norwegian hay is being taken ashore on 31 October 1950. It is deck cargo, the bales being unsheeted and manhandled by a gang of stevedores, preparing them for the sling, all under the supervision of the ganger or checker in charge.

The hay has now been stacked on the waiting road transport, and these two Austin K4s will be carrying quite a load, although not for a great distance, from Queen Alexandra Dock to Upper Boat, a small village located between Taffs Well and Rhydyfelin, about 8 miles away. At six bales high, although a fairly stable load it will still catch the wind, even though roped down tight. Canvas sheets are lashed to the top of the cab roof, so there will be those irritating little stalks of hay being deposited along the road and catching pedestrians and other traffic all the way to Noah Rees & Griffins' premises at Upper Boat!

Baulk timber is being discharged in December 1951 from a vessel direct to these coupled sets of twin bolster trucks (bearing the serial numbers 205638, 205637 and 205543). Between the bolsters and the ship can be seen a number of internal-user railway wagons, also carrying this discharged timber; the wagon on the right carries the legend 'Not to run more than 3 miles on the main lines'.

Above The SS *Fred Christensen*, flying the Norwegian national flag from her stern, is loading 'CKDs' – motor cars packed in a dismantled state, or 'completely knocked down' – from the Bedford Trucks factory on 8 August 1949, bound for General Motors, Holdens, Woodville, Adelaide, Australia. Behind the ex-LMS railway wagons the stacked crates contain Vauxhall car parts, also for export.

Below It is January 1952, and this view catches a car in mid-flight, about to be lowered into the vessel's hold. The label in this car's window reads 'British Hillman Minx', and on the ground are more waiting to use this new type of single car lifting frame.

Right Also using the single vehicle lifting frame is a Ford Prefect 100E, on its way to the hold of the SS *Port Chalmers*, en route to Australia in May 1955. The wooden crates below are full of different models, Land-Rovers, Commer trucks from the Rootes Group, Standard Vanguard cars, and Humber cars, also from Rootes. In the background can be seen A Shed, while in the centre is an Austin truck; the two British Road Services vehicles over on the left are Atkinsons, while standing in front of the Humber Cars crate is a Morris van.

Below In May 1960 here are more cars awaiting shipment, with more arriving by rail – Vauxhall Cresta PAs and Vauxhall Victor F series – all for export. Two of the ship's officers survey the scene from the top of the gangway. In the background can be seen the King's Wharf cold store, while on the extreme left is a corner of A Shed.

Above In February 1962 a batch of tractors has arrived by rail for export. In the background a Stothert & Pitt 6-ton-capacity crane is loading a Poole-manufactured 'Shawnee' trailer aboard the vessel *Lakonia* (port of registration Glasgow). Again, the A Shed complex can be seen on the left.

Below In the same month Fordson Dexta tractors are arriving, carried on a varied selection of trucks; the three nearest the camera on the left are a one-plank 'Lowfit' (No B452032) and two 'Carfits' (Nos S39421 and E203090). On the right, also awaiting export, are a batch of Austin Healey Sprite sports cars.

Alongside A Shed in around 1965, Stothert & Pitt crane No 25 is in the process of loading Ford Anglias aboard the SS *Bannercliff*, while the crane behind is loading steel coils. Nearest the camera is an ex-LMS bolster wagon, No M720508, and behind are some British Railways 'Shock' open wagons, easily identified by their white painted lines – one is No B720715. These are followed by a former LNER all-steel open wagon, a type adopted by British Railways and some of which were used in the Civil Engineers fleet.

This is the large storage area between G Shed (left) and A Shed (right); at the rear is C Shed. There was always a lot of activity in this area, and in this May 1967 view 'Buy British' is the motto. Parked in ranks are Morris Minor cars over by C Shed, with rows of MGA sports cars on the far left, Morris Minis in front and to the left and, in the centre of the Minis, a couple of Morris Oxfords. In the foreground, with their whitewall tyres evident, are Metropolitans. Next to the open area on the right are three Austin Healey Sprite sports cars. Beyond C Shed the large building is the Mountstuart-owned Channel Dry Dock. During the war years of 1944 and 1945 C Shed accommodated Canadian and American servicemen killed in the European theatres, and many hundreds of coffins and caskets were deposited in this warehouse during that terrible period.

Another view of the area between G and A Sheds, in January 1971, with C Shed and the 15-ton crane of the Channel Dry Docks in the background.

Left In September 1956 the SS *Glomdal* from Oslo is discharging her cargo of bananas to road and rail vehicles using conveyors. For shoppers used to seeing bananas in 'hands' of four or five, here are whole stalks! The ship may be one of Geest Industries' vessels, as during this period Geest was endeavouring to increase its tonnages of bananas carried from the Windward Islands to the United Kingdom, and initially random vessels from the company's home port of Preston would arrive at a weekend, discharge and leave immediately, which may be the case here. As this trade developed a dedicated berth and cold store was provided at Barry Docks, which operated for many years until the company left South Wales and set up a base at Southampton Docks in 1992.

Below More bananas are being landed at Queen Alexandra Docks on 22 January 1957. This photograph gives a clear view of G Shed with H Shed in the distance. Right of centre in this very busy scene can be seen a 'tallyman' (wearing a peaked cap) with a policeman; elsewhere there are quite a number of tallymen, as well as checkers, standing by the doorway of each of the railway vans. A former LMS Banana van can be seen next to the mobile crane; British Railways built 300 Banana vans for the conveyance of this traffic from docks to depots.

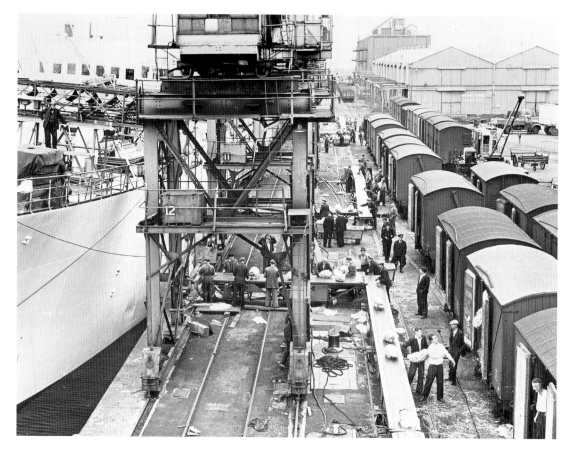

Above This is the vessel *Alexandros Koryzis* discharging wood pulp to a varied mixture of vacuum-fitted railway wagons: two ex-LMS five-plank wagons (the one on the right is No M18949) and a former LNER steel 13-ton open type, redesigned by British Railways, between them. On the right is a former Southern Railway eight-plank 13-ton open wagon, circa 1960; stencilled in white are the words 'Not to be used for P.W. ballast or other engineers materials', and the wagon carries the serial S27037.

Right Once again trestles come in useful in September 1960 – this time for a pallet of cheese, which is being discharged from a vessel direct into internal-use-only vans, all of which are former GWR ventilated vans.

Left Ingot moulds are being loaded with the help of the 50-ton floating crane in July 1961. This crane was made during wartime, its base being constructed from two barges connected together. Alongside the crane and assisting is the tugboat *Cardiff Rose*, while over on the left is a trailer for a tractor, awaiting export. Beyond is the frontage of the A Shed complex, and the vessel at berth is the *Reine Astrid*, of Göteborg, Sweden.

Below Panama pine from Brazil is being discharged from the *Cläre Hugo Stinnes* to waiting empty wagons in February 1962. On the left is a former North Eastern Railway 13-ton, six-plank wagon bearing the serial number E207125, of 6 tons 8 cwt tare, which has seen better days! Next to it is a 13-ton, 6-17 tare wagon, No M423627, of LMS origin, then a former GWR six-plank wagon, No W133189. On the right is a rake of internal-user wagons.

This GWR shunting tractor, No 199, seen here in 1946 at Queen Alexandra Dock, was built by Messrs Muir Hill of Manchester. Although not a pretty thing to look at, with its steel girder frame and solid tyres, these were mechanical workhorses that could be seen around the Great Western Railway network as well as inside the company's docks.

This Lister Auto Truck, photographed in 1951, was manufactured by R. A. Lister & Co Ltd of Dursley, Gloucestershire. The small round badge above the name at the front bears the number LT 238, while painted on the side is FT 708. This heavy-looking yet very mobile three-wheeler carries a good load of railway wagon tarpaulins.

A Chase side shovel, in use by the Cardiff Docks Civil Engineering Department, is seen here loading a truck in about 1954.

Above This Ransome-Rapier 10-ton mobile crane is conveying a boiler for shipment, circa 1958. With its solid tyres and massive counterweight, it took a skilled man to handle it. There was a number of mobile cranes used in the docks, all differing in make or lifting power. In the background is a side view of A Shed, and some Bedford trucks.

Below Also taken in 1958 near the side of A Shed, this photograph shows a Neal 2-ton mobile crane, road registration number JXD 118, being used to move crated items. Behind the crane we have a better view of the Bedford trucks awaiting shipment.

A Shed

Above We now move on to the area of Queen Alexandra Dock occupied by A Shed, the former No 1 Shed, which was also known amongst dockers as the Queen's Warehouse. This interior view was taken in March 1927, and shows sack trolleys in general use moving boxes, wooden crates and barrels. Many of the shedmen are ripping open the crates, but what is inside them remains a mystery; what is certain is that there was no shortage of work, even for the man with the sweeping brush. The men who worked inside the sheds were known as dock porters or shedmen at Cardiff, and were not registered dock workers (RDWs).

Another inside view of A Shed, in July 1927, shows fruit and general cargo stored there, amongst which can be identified boxes of Swift's 'Silverleaf' pure lard from the USA, Pedro Cascales Conservas from Spain (the sides of the boxes stamped 'Cardiff'), and sacks of sugar beside the inevitable and reliable sack trolley.

Outside A Shed wooden boxes of Jaffa oranges are being discharged from the SS *Rita Maersk*, a Maersk Line (Denmark) vessel, in November 1946. The first two open five-plank wagons on the right are both former LMS wagons.

Two dockers, well wrapped up with scarves and heavy overcoats against the biting winds that swirl about the docks, steady a pallet of boxed Jaffa oranges from the *Rita Maersk*.

Above A Ransome's electric low-loading pallet-carrier transports boxes of oranges inside A Shed in about 1954.

Below Twenty years later another cargo of Jaffa fruit is being discharged into A Shed from the *Rochester Castle*. In the doorway is a Hyster Ransomes electrically operated truck, known as a 'bogie', which, like its predecessor, took a lot of the manual work out of the task of transhipping. The cargo was carefully placed on the bogie's flat bed (or floor), the load was then raised and taken into the shed where the boxes of fruit were sorted into marks (or grades) by hand. The man operating the bogie would stand behind the box (just out of view in this photograph), and operate the forward and reverse gears, and the long steering handle. Note that a sideboard is in place half-way up the pallet, holding this rather flimsy collection of boxwood together.

Above More Jaffa oranges are being discharged from ship to British Road Services vehicles in about 1960. The lorry in the centre, an AEC Mammoth Major Mk 3 belonging to an unidentified BRS depot, is being loaded with oranges, while on the right, partially hidden, is the flatbed of another BRS vehicle, with an Aberdeen depot trailer attached. On the left some of the cargo ('Jaffa Lates', ie fruit that ripens late in the season, probably oranges) will be stored in A Shed. Each pallet and box is being accounted for by the men standing, watching and checking from their elevated position on the loading bay. In 1963 *Ship Ahoy* magazine reported: 'The first of this season's imports of citrus fruit was handled at Cardiff Docks in January, when 32,000 cases of oranges and grapefruits from Israel were unloaded from the Norwegian *Haukefjell* for distribution throughout South Wales and the West Country.'

Left Another perishable cargo, sacks of Canadian potatoes, are being unloaded into a line-up of road vehicles in June 1947. The ship belongs to the Canadian Pacific Steamship Company Ltd, which operated routes to London, Liverpool and the continent from Canada and the USA; it also ran a service from London to the Great Lakes of Canada. The lorries are, from left to right, a Chevrolet, a Guy Vixant and a Dodge.

The SS *Baron Ramsay* is discharging sugar to A Shed in May 1949; it looks as though some is also going into railway wagons. The nearest wagon has been sheeted to protect the cargo from rain, while that in front is being prepared to receive the cargo.

The sacks of sugar are being loaded from A Shed into a railway wagon via a Spencer mobile conveyor belt, bearing the number ME 2119. The former 13-ton LNER 'High Steel' wagon is No 278910.

Meanwhile, inside A Shed the electrical elevators certainly help to protect the cargo and the shedmen from harm. The sugar is being stacked nearly 30 bags high!

Left A cargo of tomatoes from the SS *Cilicia* is stacked inside A Shed in April 1950; those on the left are labelled 'Arosa', and those on the right 'Canary Islands Produce'. Note the 'No Smoking' sign prominent on the whitewashed wall of the building, as a reminder that sometimes this building stored more than just tomatoes.

Below More fruit: the SS *Banaderos* is discharging Brazilian oranges onto waiting pallets on the loading bay outside A Shed on 10 April 1951. Early rain has finished, leaving puddles on the bay. Dock porters are awaiting the first boxes to be discharged, and soon they will be inside A Shed; already at least one man has grabbed a sack truck. Between the men and the crane is a rake of five-plank open wagons; stencilled on the nearest one is 'Empty to Newport (Alexandra Dock Junction)'. All the wagons are carrying heavy lengths of bulk timber. At berth behind the *Banaderos* is the *Sardia*.

Above In this busy scene captured on 31 October 1950 bales of Norwegian hay are being unloaded into waiting railway vehicles, and parties of men are working hard inside the wagons, stacking the hay as it is lowered, while others are making use of wooden ladders to climb inside and prepare the next wagon for its share of hay, or to pull tarpaulin sheets over to cover the load before the weather changes. One group of dockers are taking a few minutes' breather – they have covered their wagons, which is not easy work. Note that, with all the hay that is being handled, very little is scattered about.

Right Looking out of place inside A Shed in July 1951 are at least four eye-catching MG TD Midget motor cars, tucked in between barrels, crates, bags and other items under the heading of 'miscellaneous general cargo'.

Left Cars have taken over completely in this interior view of A Shed, awaiting export to South Africa in June 1948. The car in the centre is a Jaguar, and the two behind are Armstrong Siddeleys, while the first car in the row behind, next to the supporting pillar, is a Citroen Light 15. All these motor cars are gleaming new and well beyond the purse of a hard-working docker, most of whom came to work on pushbikes, caught the bus, or just walked.

Below left Nearby in the C Shed complex in the same month quite a collection of cars are again awaiting export to South Africa. On the extreme right is a Singer Nine Roadster, then a Humber, with the same makes repeated along the rows. The roof of this buildings was lined with the sides of ammunition boxes.

Right Back in A Shed, in May 1951, more cars are awaiting shipment overseas, and they are beauties! All are MG TD sport cars, with the exception of some Morris Minors and Hillman Minxes, and all are left-hand drive.

Below This is A Shed again, circa 1956, with Austin A40 Devons en route to Canada; the windscreen stickers read 'The Austin Motor Co (Canada) Ltd, Vancouver BC' or simply 'Canada'. A Shed was handy, being near to the dockside, which meant less time wasted, and being under cover kept these cars in the same pristine condition in which they had arrived.

Above In August 1958 we see a part consignment of motor cars, again for shipment overseas. In the bottom right-hand corner is a Vauxhall Cresta PA with a windscreen sticker reading 'Export'. The other models seem to be Series 2 Hillman Minxes, two of which have windscreen stickers with 'USA' printed on them.

Below Arriving by rail in August 1958 is a rake of Vauxhall Victor F Series cars on 'Lowfit' railway trucks, one of which carries the serial E184443. The cars are en route to the hold of the MV *Hawke* for export abroad. In the right background, caught on camera as it is hoisted aboard, are the unmistakable features of a Metropolitan motor car.

we lads bagged the registration number and the make of car, and gazed with awe at the polished leather upholstery and wooden steering wheels, or played amongst even older cars that were rusting in a scrapyard or had just been left for chickens to roost in, abandoned on an allotment site, or on a local farmer's land, before going home with dreams of 'some day...', only to be brought back to reality with a cold meal and a penetrating sentence from Mum: 'Where have you been?' Here we have an Austin A40 Countryman van and a Triumph Renown saloon, en route with others to Canada in May 1951.

Below Outside A Shed on the loading bay on 4 August 1950 is a new specially improved version of the single car axle hoist, known as 'spreaders', seen here being tried out on what looks like a special job, an Austin Shearline motor car, which will probably be shipped as deck cargo.

Below right Suspended for a few moments before entering the hold of the SS *Stankeld*, we have a chance to witness a time when these cars were a daily sight on our roads, when

Left Seen a few years earlier, in October 1947, this single axle sling seems less sophisticated than the type seen in the previous pictures, yet was probably just as efficient. A Ford Anglia is being taken aboard the SS *Turkistan*, one of the Frank C. Strickland Company vessels and part of the P & O general cargo division of London, whose routes ran from the UK and the continent to the Persian Gulf.

Below Having emerged from A Shed in May 1951, this Hillman Minx is being carried in a 'spreader' and is midway across towards the hold of the SS *Stankeld*, while in a more distant doorway another car is being prepared. It seems that the axle supports must project sufficiently for the chains of the 'spreader' not to damage the bodywork of the cars, and 'palliasse' bags, as seen previously, are not needed.

Right The north side of Queen Alexandra Dock also accommodated passenger ships. This is the RMS *St Hillary* embarking passengers and luggage for West Africa in September 1946. The GWR Express Cartage Services vehicle in the foreground is a Thornycroft, and carrying advertisements on the sides of the company's road vehicles was an accepted practise, which went on into British Railway days. The loading bay platform establishes the location as opposite A Shed. The Passenger Terminus for this vessel was at the end of C Shed, near the B Shed side; however, passengers had to walk through this shed to reach the passenger vessel berth, which was alongside mooring bollard No 24.

Below The SS *Jol Azad* (port of registration Bombay) disembarks its passengers at Empire Wharf in June 1949 as they start a new life in a new land. A former GWR wagon provides a handy support for the gangway. Note the lifeboats, neatly stored on their davits, using the gravity principle of release.

Above In May 1960 the tug *Lord Glanely* is giving assistance to floating cranes that are discharging a heavy cargo over the vessel's side. Beyond the tug is the 50-ton floating crane constructed during the Second World War to Ministry of War Transport specifications, while in the distance can be seen the 100-ton floating crane *Simson III*, of Dutch manufacture. The tug is one of the docks' oldest vessels, and the addition of the lifeboat was necessary to meet safety requirements. These floating cranes would be manned by three or four men, who would be augmented by one or two others to assist with moving lines, depending on the crane's demands. Moulds and ingots of this type would be beyond the lifting capacity of the dockside cranes, so the floating cranes provided a convenient means of handling them while the dockside cranes handled the rest of the cargo aboard the *Kurt Arlt*.

Left The ingot moulds are being lowered onto 'Borail WG' wagons; placing the weight as close to this bolster wagons' bogies as possible will help to give extra support to the load.

Above This is the newly erected A Shed extension, as seen from the deck of the SS *City of Oxford* in July 1961. Nearest the camera are pit props stacked inside an open steel-sided British Railways wagon built to a former LNER design; it is part of a rake of three-plank open wagons all carrying pit props. Alongside is another line of railway wagons, of various sizes and being loaded with sacks. In the left-hand doorway of the extension is a British Road Services Leyland, and in front of it a Morris J Type van and a Ford Anglia motor car. The other BRS lorry, an eight-wheel Bristol HG6, is from the Melksham depot, whose name and fleet number have been applied to the side. This area later became the site for the new F Shed, built in 1980.

Left In 1968 aluminium sheet is being unloaded onto Plate wagons from the vessel *Teinaron* via a mobile rail-mounted crane.

Left A bird's-eye view of a ship's hold filled to capacity with International 434 tractors made at the International Harvester factory in Doncaster. This factory was established in 1939, but it was not until 1949 that production started on their first British-made tractor.

Sawmills area

Below This aerial view of 6 August 1970 shows clearly the former sawmills area, with the corner into the Communication Passage and Bell's Wharf. The berthed vessel is being prepared to take on board a cargo of motor cars for export. On the left A Shed and the new A Shed extension are clearly seen, and behind them is B Shed, to the right of which are the remains of the sawmill complex; the former wood storage and drying shed have gone, giving more area for storage, in this case a gigantic car park. In 2006 the area where the vessel is berthed was part of Marshall's Maritime Services, which has since moved. Where the cars are parked, near the A Shed extension, is where the new F Shed was built in 1980 (in use today as a common-user shed). Today Bell's Wharf is part of the Cardiff Forest Products Group, handling timber products. In the top right-hand corner can just be glimpsed the Communications Passage swing bridge, and what looks like the 50-ton MOWT floating crane. To the left is the Crown Fuel Works, and left again, on the quayside of Roath Basin, is Messrs Bowles Sand Wharf.

Below right Car transporters are bringing more cars for export in May 1967. The British Road Services car transporter is from the Oxford depot, with its number, 4G409, next to the lion, wheel and crown emblem of this nationalised service; it is carrying the ever-popular Mini. Beyond is another transporter carrying Austin Metropolitan motor cars.

Below The area between the Sawmill and the Crown Fuel Works is just about filled to capacity in May 1967. This is Bell's Wharf, and the Pierhead Building can be seen on the skyline; number of sheerleg cranes can also be seen, and a mobile road crane is next to the sawmill's doors. The higher and lower level coaling lines can be seen in the middle distance, while the building on the right is the Pump House. Buses for export are lined up on the right, and the rest of the vehicles are British-made motor cars awaiting export all over the world: the front right-hand group are Ford Cortina Mk IIs, while the other larger group consist of, left to right, more Mk II Cortinas, Triumph GT 6s, Vauxhall Viva HBs, and another batch of Cortinas.

Right Seen from a crane window in September 1967 is a line-up of single-decker buses en route to South America and destined for the Jamaica Omnibus Service. Immediately behind them are Ford Cortina Mk IIs and Triumph Spitfire sports cars, also ready for export. Prominent at the front of the rear group are two white Triumph GT6s, contrasting with the Morris Minor and Ford Classic in the right foreground, which would certainly belong to dockers.

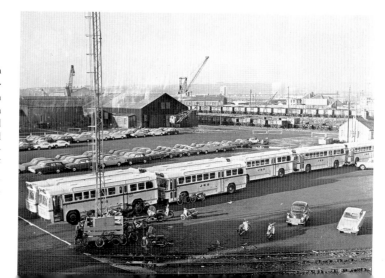

Above In this second view from September 1967, in the background is the Crown Fuel Works, and at the end of the row of cranes (Nos 21-24) can just be seen the end of the Communication Bridge; I estimate that we must be at the window of No 19. Beside No 23 is the Cardiff tugboat *Ebbw*. The cars in the background are Ford Cortina Mk II saloons and estate, with Jaguars in the nearest row. The cars to the right of the mechanical shunter mainly consist of E Type Jaguars, with Jaguar Mk 10s at the back and Rover 2000 series at the near end. The car in the foreground is a Morris 1100, behind which is a Vauxhall Viva HB. On the extreme right can be seen the axle hoist equipment. In the background on the extreme left is a Commer PB pick-up van, then in the left foreground are more Ford Cortina Mk IIs, Hillman Minxes and Triumph sports cars.

Left The JOS buses are now stowed on the ship's deck, ready to begin their journey. The visible destination blind reads 'Champion House' and 'Brentford Road'. On the other side are two doors; the rear folding doors are labelled 'Pay as you enter' and the front door (opposite the driver) is the 'Exit'. On the front of each bus is an emblem of a torch surrounded by a laurel wreath with wings on either side, in the centre of which is the word 'Olympic'.

Above A few years earlier, this is a general view of the dockside in August 1956. On the left is a timber storage building, part of the sawmill complex, constructed of wood with gaps between allowing ventilation to dry out the timber stored within. Planks of sawn wood are stacked alongside, out in the open, in the midst of which a group of men are taking a break Note that the electrically operated capstans are painted white, remnants of wartime blackout regulations. On the right is the SS *Jaljawahar* (port of registration Bombay), and the dockside cranes are discharging her cargo of crushed bones to waiting road vehicles – a Leyland followed by an unrecognisable BRS vehicle, then a Proctor and a Bedford and, to its right, a Maudsley. Beyond them open railway wagons are full of sawn planks of timber.

Above right In about 1970 the *Floristan*, one of the Frank C. Strickland Co vessels, is berthed alongside three quayside cranes; the two on the right are by Stothert & Pitt, while the one on the left may be a Babcock & Wilson crane. The crane on the right is of a standard 3-ton lift, with the other two are possibly 6 tons. At the base of the cranes is a rake of Bogie Bolster C wagons in the centre of which is an open five-plank Tube wagon. In December 1970 *Harbour Lights* magazine recorded that the newest addition to the Strick Line, the 9,627-ton cargo liner *Nigaristan*, had arrived at Cardiff Docks on 9 October, where she loaded general cargo for her maiden voyage to Arabian and Iranian ports. The *Nigaristan*, which

cost £2¼ million, was built by the Redhead division of Swan Hunter, and was the 46th to be built at South Shields for Stricks and the sixth company vessel to bear the name. She had been launched the previous June by Mrs Barbara James, wife of Mr P. H. James, a director of Frank C. Strickland & Co (South Wales), and was delivered a month ahead of schedule. She brought to 18 the size of the Strick fleet of fast cargo liners operating the Strick and Ellerman service to the Persian Gulf. In command of the *Nigaristan* on her maiden voyage was Captain S. A. Booker, a member of a Barry seafaring family and Commodore of the Fleet, who had joined the company as a cadet in 1922.

Above Cargo is being loaded aboard the *Armanistan* on 3 July 1968 from Hyster Ransomes platform trucks. Also in view are the legs of a DD2-type crane.

Below Another of the newly purchased DD2 cranes, of 7½-ton lifting capacity, is photographed hoisting a former London Transport bus (an AEC RT) towards the deck of the waiting vessel en route to the USA, destined for 'Ye Olde Kansas City Touring Assn Ltd'.

By 1971 these DD2 cranes were gradually replacing the older type of crane, and seen here are some of the 7½-ton portal cranes in action, hoisting a batch of tractors aboard the *Cornelia Maersk*.

A Register Card (still headed 'GWR') for a Stothert & Pitt movable electric portal crane, the prototype DD2/1, purchased in July 1971 at a cost of £5,500 second-hand from the Port of London Authority. As a result of negotiation, this represented the cost of the crane in situ at London Docks, and would not necessarily include the cost of moving it from London to Cardiff. It had originally been the PLA's E1000 at Surrey Docks, and was built in 1959 with a 5-ton lift.

Left and below left On 13 June 1971 the floating crane *Simson III* lifts the Hawker Siddeley diesel-electric locomotive prototype, No HS4000 *Kestrel*, off its bogies before taking it to the waiting Russian vessel *Kpachokamck*, assisted by the tugs *Butegarth* and *Danegarth*, to be exported to the USSR. According to *Harbour Lights* magazine, during the second weekend in January 1971 there had been no fewer than five Russian vessels in Cardiff at the same time, an indication of how the Russians were rapidly expanding into the world's sea trade. Another, the Cypriot-registered *Petros*, had been hit by a series of misfortunes on its way from Russia to Cardiff with a cargo of pit props, and had been 'arrested' at Cardiff Docks under a writ issued by the Admiralty Marshal. The trouble started for the 1,786-ton vessel when she ran out of fuel on her journey from Archangel. Her cargo shifted in a storm and she developed an 18-degree list to port due to partial loss of the deck cargo, which caused the remaining pit props to shift. She ran aground on Bressay (Shetland Isles) and was towed to Lerwick, then to Aberdeen, where she was struck by two other vessels. After a lengthy period in Aberdeen she was towed to Cardiff Docks by German tugs on 20 January 1971.

Right After loading his Dodge K Series with boxes of Jaffa oranges, the driver is now tidying up his load before sheeting it over and roping it off in February 1973. The lorry is at the rear of A Shed, and in the distance can be seen the taller extension. Beyond the Dodge is a unit and trailer belonging to British Rail, whose new logo can be seen on the trailer; beyond again is an ERF LV. On the left is the brickwork of B Shed, outside which is a tractor and a Ford D Series lorry. The railway line running between the sheds was known as the compound line.

Communication Passage and Empire Wharf

Once past the timber yards, at the top-most corner of Queen Alexandra Dock, is Communication Passage with its swing bridge. The Passage is 590 feet in length by 90 feet wide. A steel caisson was constructed to fit both the caisson sills of the Passage and the Entrance Lock, to be used in either location as necessity required.

Opposite Bell's Wharf and the timber yards was Schroeters Wharf, another massive timber area, which subsequently became known as Empire Wharf. Later a transit shed was built here, but by the 1990s it had gone, and by 2003 the wharf was being used by RMC Aggregates. Today the wharf is jointly used by RMC and Hanson's Aggregates (the latter has a batching plant in this area, but uses the north side of Roath Dock, with UMA, for sand discharge).

Right In about 1932 a mountain of pit props is being stored and will subsequently be despatched to the collieries as required.

Below Another way of stacking pit props was the 'birdcage' method, alternating the direction of each layer and thus improving stability, as seen here again in about 1932. Usually this wood was imported from Scandinavian countries as well as Russia and the Baltic States.

The ice factory vessel *Tunisie* is believed to be at berth in Queen Alexandra Dock is September 1934. It was an unusual visitor to South Wales, normally serving the deep-sea fishing fleet.

Hay rakes are lined up ready for shipping into the hold of the SS *Nailsea Moor* in November 1945, part of a United Nations Relief & Rehabilitation Aid programme to assist war-ravaged Yugoslavia.

This threshing machine was part of the same cargo. Powered by a portable steam traction engine, it would separate the heads from the crop to produce about a ton of grain per hour.

Above This is the girder swing bridge across the Communication Passage, also known as Compass bridge, on 27 June 1987. Ryan's coal-blending dump can be seen in the background near Roath Dock Inner Lock, and beyond is evidence of the re-development of the Cardiff Bay area. The small red-brick building in the foreground was probably used for the safe storage of maintenance materials. *Author*

Below This is Empire Wharf, with its transit shed and quayside cranes beside Communication Passage in about 1946, looking north-west. In the background can be seen vessels in Roath Dock and the sidings feeding the coaling cranes on the south side of that dock, beyond which are the tall chimneys of the steelworks. On the right is the area known as the 'Prairie', mainly used during the war years for the storage of United States war equipment.

Above A general view of the two side-by-side transit sheds at Empire Wharf, looking in the opposite direction circa 1953. The 'Beware of Trains' sign is a reminder of the real danger from railway traffic, which was everywhere in those days, steam hissing and trucks clanking, and accidents were never far off. Three insulated meat vans can be seen beyond the notice, two of Southern Railway vintage and the one in the centre of LMS design.

Left Looking north-west again, in August 1946, Lewis Hunter luffing cranes are unloading Brazilian oranges from the SS *Olav Bakke*, some of which are going into railway vans. On board the vessel a member of the crew is on a hoist painting or cleaning the funnel, and on deck in the bottom left-hand corner, standing alongside one of the motors for operating the derrick, two of the ship's crew are talking to one of its officers. On the wall of the transit shed is a GWR First Aid cabinet.

Above Inside the Empire Wharf transit shed, an open railway wagon stands in the bay beside boxes of Brazilian oranges, part of the cargo of the SS *Olav Bakke* in August 1946.

Right Busy as usual in the 1950s, boxes of 'Astra' Jaffa grapefruit are being unloaded on to Empire Wharf en route for storage into the nearby transit shed. In the distance the smoke from the Crown Fuel Works hangs heavy in the air. The ship carries the quadrant type of lifeboat davits.

Left The enormous power of the docks' 100-ton floating crane *Simson III* is seen here as it suspends this steel melting furnace in mid-air. The furnace was manufactured by GWB Furnaces Ltd of Dudley, Worcestershire, for export to Canada, circa 1950.

Below Here is another view of *Simson III* in action, assisted by the steam tugboat *The Earl* on 20 September 1950. It is lifting a 75-ton English Electric transformer away from the quayside to be placed into the hold of the SS *Cid*; the transformer was made at the company's Stafford works.

On the loading dock (staging) at Empire Wharf in May 1951, the SS *Antenusia* is discharging bags of barley directly into railway wagons. To gain height the docker has used two trestles, one on top of the other, to get the sacks into former GWR van No W79241.

Inside the Empire Wharf transit shed, circa 1953, is a complete shipment of Austin Loadstar trucks awaiting export – they bring to mind those African safari films!

In fact, the trucks are destined not for Africa, but to assist in reconstruction work in war-damaged Korea in the aftermath of the 1950-53 Korean War. This conflict finally ended with the restoration of the agreed boundary at the 38th parallel, which to this day separates the Communist Democratic People's Republic of Korea in the north from the Republic of Korea in the south. In the background can be seen one of the two transit sheds at Empire Wharf.

Above A luffing crane is using an 'octopus' (or 'spider') grab to discharge scrap iron from the SS *Irish Hazel* into a waiting rake of open railway wagons in May 1955; the wagon with the man alongside bears the number S9569. The scrap is destined for the nearby Dowlais Works of GKN. These 'octopus' grabs were the standard means of loading and unloading cargoes of scrap iron and were robust enough to break into the interlocked mass of metal; quayside cranes would be modified at a reasonable cost to operate with them. When magnetic equipment became available, there was not only a substantial cost involved, but also a resistance from the ship operators because of the adverse effect they would have on the ship's instruments and electrics.

Above Berthed alongside Empire Wharf, the *Colombia*, from Göteborg in Sweden, is discharging timber and hardboard into waiting road and rail wagons in February 1962. The railway wagons are a mixture of six- and seven-plank open wagons and at least one former LNER steel one, while to the right of the wagons stands a British Road Services Leyland Beaver.

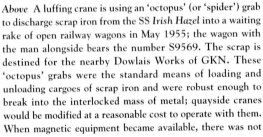

Left It is February 1962, and the Aden campaign has begun. At the rear of the Empire Wharf transit sheds is a back-to-back line-up of British Army Bedford RLs, while in the background there is also a strong military presence. The lorries are marshalled and awaiting shipment, with headlights taped over and details, including the destination of Aden, stencilled on the cab doors. The circular ring on the cab roofs, with a canvas cover in place, is where a machine-gun will be attached. In the left background is the Communication Passage, and on the right the tall empty building is all that remains of the Coal Washery.

King's Wharf

The top (north-eastern) end of Queen Alexandra Dock is known as King's Wharf, the location of a cold store commenced in 1940 by the Ministry of Food, and one of the most modern in the country. By the 1950s this was under the control of National Cold Stores (Management) Ltd, and managed by the British Transport Commission. It was a steel-framed brick structure of five floors, comprising 26 chambers in six sections of approximately equal size, equipped with nine 2-ton electric lifts. The total refrigerated space provided was 1,018,612 cubic feet, capable of accommodating about 10,000 tons of goods. The store was built alongside a deep-water berth, and was served by both rail and road for the speedy receiving and distribution of refrigerated cargoes.

In addition to meat, the store handled butter, cheese, eggs, fish and other foodstuffs requiring cold storage accommodation.

By 1978 the cold store was known as the International Cold Storage. In 1990 the 'A' engine house, which was part of the building and provided the power for the freezers and lifts to the floors, was demolished, leaving 'B' engine house to cope alone. Other parts of the cold store were demolished between 1990 and 1993. The remaining part of the building was rebuilt, partly on the demolished area of the old one in 1993, and this ongoing programme of extensions and improvements continued right up to 1996, at a cost to ABP of £1 million. Another cold store was built alongside in 2003, thus effectively providing the dock with a completely new cold storage complex; it is officially listed as an EU border import post.

The SS *Charlton Hall* is discharging sawn timber at King's Wharf into open railway wagons, circa 1947.

Below Berthed at King's Wharf is the Swedish vessel SS *Hornberg*, discharging lumber from the Bahamas, varying from sawn planks to large lengths of pit wood, circa 1947. Note that this vessel is carrying her lifeboat in the radial type of davit. In the background is the *Indian Exporter* at Bell's Wharf, and beyond it in the far distance is the Bute Dry Dock building.

Bottom In April 1947 the SS *Wairangi* discharging perishable goods into the nearby King's Wharf cold store and barrels of cheese into the railway wagons and road transport waiting below. In this very busy scene, scattered around are sack trucks and wooden trestles, and alongside the loading dock (nearest the camera) is a loose-coupled GWR Iron van.

Right Circa 1948 frozen meat and general cargo are being discharged from the SS *Port Huon* onto manual trolleys en route to the cold store for packing and storage.

Below right If the previous photograph showed a busy scene, here is an even busier one! It is May 1949 and the SS *Urmston Grange* is discharging frozen meat at King's Wharf. Removing the carcases from the netting is busy work; using temporary tables to do the job is an excellent method, involving less back-aching bending. Once out of the net, the meats goes straight onto the trolley and inside the cold store, onto lifts and into the chill room, quick and direct. Some of this cargo is destined for the insulated railway vans and containers, a combination of former SR and GWR vehicles and, on the right, a 10-ton LMS Steam Banana van. Over on the left, in the distance, a signal box is silhouetted against the skyline.

Left This photograph of the SS *Port Sydney* discharging meat and dairy products in about 1955 provides a broader view of King's Wharf and its cold store.

Below left This photograph overlooking Bell's Wharf was taken from the cold store in about 1960. The vessel in the foreground is one of the Port Line ships that ran between the United Kingdom and New Zealand and Australia via the Cape. Note the winch motors on the forecastle deck, which operate the ship's anchors. At berth at Bell's Wharf are a number of ships; the one in the centre is the *Mostun* (port of registration Kristiansand), beyond which is a small coaster, possibly a Bristol Steam Navigation Co vessel.

Right In September 1960 drivers work to load their vehicles as quickly as possible. All are BRS vehicles – at the front are two AEC Mercurys, and behind them an AEC Mammoth Major, while the last two may be another pair of Mercurys. The nearest crane is No 31, followed by Nos 30 and 29, all busy unloading boxes of New Zealand butter onto the road and railway wagons as well as onto the cold store loading dock. On the boxes is written 'New Zealand for creamier butter'.

Below In another view of this busy loading dock, circa 1960, New Zealand frozen lamb is being handled. Note the protective muslin cloth wrappers; when I worked as a butcher this cloth was brilliant, and had a multitude of additional uses, as a polisher, strainer, dish cloth, and window cloth. On the left are a number of insulated containers on 'Lowfit' wagons, while on the right are some internal-user ex-GWR vans being loaded with boxed cheese.

This unusual view was taken from the roof of the cold store, and looking down we see demolition work in progress – only the staging remains of what was once the Empire Wharf warehouses. The roof in the foreground (showing the slatted construction of the cooling equipment) is part of 'A' engine house. The quayside cranes are discharging a cargo of wood pulp into British Railways vacuum-fitted open wagons, all of which are marked 'XP', allowing use in express trains. The vessel has an all-welded hull, which means that it is probably of wartime construction. Over at Bell's Wharf can be seen the overhead conveyor belt, part of the Crown Fuel Works complex.

To:- THE GREAT WESTERN RAILWAY COMPANY.

WE, VICKERS-ARMSTRONGS LIMITED of VICKERS HOUSE BROADWAY
WESTMINSTER LONDON S.W.1 IN CONSIDERATION or your hiring
to us for short periods your number 5 MOORING BARGE Now lying
at CARDIFF hereby accept and acknowledge delivery of the same
complete and in seaworthy condition and we hereby agree to
pay you in advance the sum of SIX GUINEAS per day or part of
a day by way of rent for such hire this to include the services
of the Winchman and Fireman attached to the Barge such rent
being also payable for time occupied in towing Barge from and
to point of user no charge being made for the intervening periods
when the Barge is not being used and AGREE AND UNDERTAKE to
re-deliver the same to you at CARDIFF upon the expiration of the
said period in as good working order and condition as it now is
and at our expense it being understood that the charges for
towage from and to CARDIFF are to be paid by hirers AND WE
FURTHER AGREE AND UNDERTAKE ourselves to make no claim against you
but to be responsible for and save harmless and indemnify you
from and against all actions claims losses and expenses whatsoever
in respect of loss of life or personal injury or loss of or
damage to property howsoever caused which may happen during the
period of or may arise or may in any way be attributable to the
hiring of the said Barge including claims for salvage and towage
and claims under the Workmen's Compensation Acts and Employers'
Liability Act or otherwise.

Signature of Hirer ....
Date ....

Witness :- Name ....
Address ....
Occupation ....

Above This unusually peaceful scene, circa 1954, shows the *Wedmore* of Bristol, a canal or river barge, probably fitted with a diesel engine. It has arrived at King's Wharf to pick up a cargo of New Zealand butter. On the right, placed out of harm's way and complete with protective cover, is the vessel's small boat, and just visible behind the *Wedmore* is a companion barge, probably also with a cargo of butter aboard.

Above A GWR hiring agreement form for use of a mooring barges, circa 1930. *Author's collection*

Right This rarely seen view is the rear of the cold store, circa 1947. A varied line-up of road vehicles are parked at the staging, or loading bay, area, while on the left is a GWR Steam Banana van, No 96420.

Above King's Wharf and its new cold store – one of two – are seen on Sunday 23 April 2006. At berth is the *Welsh Piper*, and over on Bell's Wharf to the left can be seen the new F Shed. *Author*

Below This is a rear view of the new cold stores photographed on the same day. The one on the right largely occupies the original site, while on the left is the new cold store extension. The sign board is for the RMC premises on Empire Wharf, and next to it is the road that leads to the quayside frontage of King's Wharf. The single-track railway line runs alongside Cold Stores Road and eventually becomes a companion to Longships Road. Today established firms and small business premises have sprung up alongside Viking Place and Longships Road, taking advantage of the security offered by the docks, including Tircon Concrete, Biffa, Atkins Trade, TIP (Trailer International Pool), Amode, Ascus Concrete, CPS, HPC, John Ford & Sons (scrap metal), and Ultra Ltd, who operate a test track and testing area for driverless taxis. *Author*

Top Behind the cold store was the 'pit prop stacking ground', as seen on this OS map, which shows the area before the cold store was built. The *GWR Magazine* of 1932 stated that, 'In order to centralise the storage of pit props at Cardiff Docks, a new site is to be prepared on land at present vacant, to the south-east of the Coal Washery at Roath Dock.' To the north ran the Cardiff Railway's line, which passed the coal washery, owned in 1922 by the Cardiff Washed Coal Company. Near to this complex were sidings holding hundreds of privately owned colliery wagons destined for the docks. *Crown copyright*

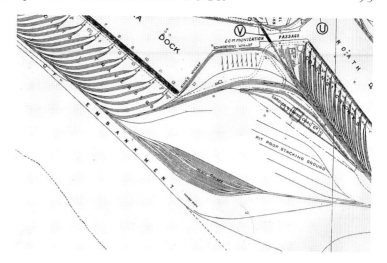

Middle A sea of pit props stretches away towards the coaling tips and cranes of Roath Dock, while on the right are at least two former LMS and GWR open wagons, circa 1932.

Bottom South of the stacking area, on land reclaimed some years previously from salt marshes, was an extensive area known as Beach Sidings. On 26 October 1947 a number of bogie vehicles waiting on the sidings carrying steel pipes for shipment to Iran as part of the Iranian Oil Pipeline; nearest the camera is a GWR Bogie Bolster C No 81813. The 1960s not only saw a boom in timber, but oil imports were also growing fast, so this area became useful as the location of oil storage tanks. By 1982 the area, which also included the Roath storage sidings and marshalling sidings, was up for development, and became home to the oil tanks of Gulf Oil

Ltd, then the Continental Oil Co Ltd, Air Products Ltd (oxygen plant) and the Ore Stacking Ground (located along Rover Way) – the latter is now Cardiff Heliport.

South side: coal staithes

Returning to the Entrance Lock, we now move up the south (strictly south-eastern) side of Queen Alexandra Dock. In 1908 we would pass eight coaling hoists, each with two coaling roads, and the ever-present weighbridges. Then there were six coaling cranes each fed by two roads. The 1922 Ordnance Survey map (page 10) shows 11 coaling hoists at the lower half of the south side, each fed by two roads and splitting into three roads at the hoist end. Beyond these are ten movable coaling cranes, each again fed by two roads, and finally, at the top end of the south side, a solitary fixed crane (see the map opposite).

In 1932 the *Great Western Railway Magazine* stated:

> Twelve new 3-ton electric luffing cranes have been provided at Queen Alexandra Dock. Also two most useful new 20-ton traverser hoists have been erected at the northern end, and brought into commission. A further three similar hoists are now in course of erection, and these will be completed and ready for use early in 1932.

According to the 1946 OS map (page 13) there are 12 traversing coal hoists numbered consecutively along the whole length of the south side of the docks. By the 1957 map (page 2) these traverser coal hoists are marked as 'movable coal hoists'. However, during the early part of the 1960s the coal trade at the docks ceased, the coaling equipment went to the scrap yard, and the tracks were lifted. In August 1962 *Ship Ahoy* magazine reported that one of Cardiff's coal hoists had been shipped by a BTC 100-ton floating crane to Swansea, to replace the No 15 tip on the north side of Kings Dock there. In August 1964 the same publication reported:

> When the *Farringay*, a small coaster, left Cardiff with 380 tons of coal on Tuesday 25 August she brought to an end the port's association with the coal trade. It was this trade that helped Cardiff to grow from a fishing village to a port known the world over, with an export peak in 1913 of 10½ million tons.

The last coal tipped at Cardiff was to bunker the tug *Exegarth* on 28 August.

The area then became a temporary scene of desolation, but times were changing, and from 1965 the area was levelled in preparation for the new timber market, mainly handled by road haulage, which from the 1960s and into the 1970s was emerging from its infancy.

In the summer of 1968 *Ship Ahoy* magazine reported:

> On March 30th the *Columbialand* (1967, 17,437gt) docked with 25,000 tons of timber, for part discharge at the new timber wharf in the Queen Alexandra Dock, Cardiff. The *Columbialand* has a beam of 87 feet 5 inches, and is the widest vessel to navigate the 90-feet lock entrance.

Two years later *Harbour Lights* magazine recorded:

> At Cardiff, the largest bulk timber carrier to enter the port arrived on 19 May 1970. She is *Sangstad* (1966, 21,596gt), which discharged 6,500 standards of packaged lumber and 200 tons of plywood. *Sangstad* was diverted from Newport due to the restriction on the length of vessels entering the latter lock. Also diverted from Newport to Cardiff was the *James Benedict* (1964, 18,123gt); she, too, had a timber cargo...
> Cardiff dockers have set a new record for the port, in the discharging of packaged lumber from the *Vancouver Forest* (1969, 17,659gt) – five gangs of dockers unloaded 1,800 standards in one day, a record average of 24.82 standards per gang/hour.

By the 1980s, Queen's Dock, as it was by then known, was destined for better things. The lower half of the south side was to become the site for new berths, with Fletchers Wharves Ltd taking over the other half. Only one new building could be seen, later known as I Shed, and used by Duferco UK Ltd. By the early years of the 21st century Longships Road had been built from a roundabout near the tank farm and the Texaco oil terminal area, heading southwards and skirting the edge of the former salt marshes to reach a junction

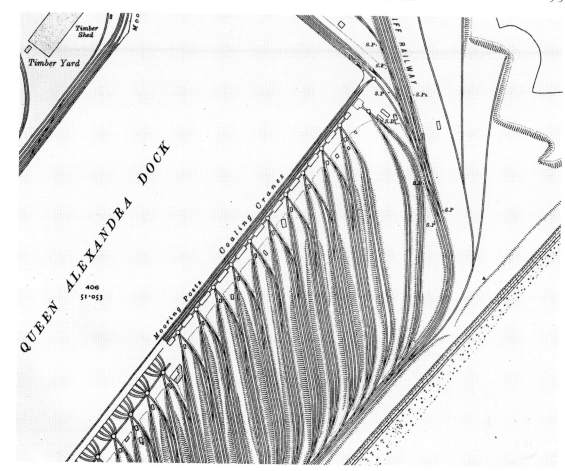

Above An Ordnance Survey map of 1920 showing the upper end of the south side of Queen Alexandra Dock and the numerous coal running roads. *Crown Copyright*

Below A corresponding general view of the coaling tips and running roads, circa 1920, from a general port booklet of 1922.

with Queens Road South, a short distance from the inner lock gates, with FAMM alongside.

Today, running parallel with Queens Road South, is the Oil Berth (see the map on page 14). At the start of this fairly short stretch of dockside road we come to the Cardiff Distribution Terminal shed (L Shed), behind which and parallel with Longships Road (opposite the FAMM complex) is the Bob Martin Terminal shed (G Shed). At the end of Queens Road South is J Shed, and to its right is K Shed; this is the Cardiff Forest Products Terminus, which handles timber logs, panel boards, paper, and pallet wood from a variety of countries, including Russia, Latvia, Scotland and Finland. We then come to the aforementioned I Shed, of Duferco UK Ltd, after which is M Shed, and the Coastal Containers terminal, with its ship-to-shore gantry cranes; this firm, part of the Coastal Containers shipping line, continues to develop new business, and now has two sailings

per week to Dublin and one to Belfast, with regular services to and from the Mediterranean. It also benefits from a daily EWS Enterprise rail service. Not far away is King's Wharf and its cold store, now operated by ABP's Connect Division, at the end of Cold Store Road. Located behind it are the buildings of Messrs Denny Matt & Dickson.

The 2003 map also shows the railway line heading from its stop blocks at the outer Entrance Lock channel, past the rear of the HCB Energy plant and FAMM before crossing Longships Road and running between the sheds and the road towards the rear of the Coastal Containers premises. Here the line turns left, leaving the roadside to head towards Cold Stores Road, crossing the waste ground that once housed the coal washery and pit prop storage areas, passing H Shed, the Cardiff Stevedores headquarters, and Jeff Dennett's steel haulage firm as it heads towards the south side of Roath Dock and beyond.

In 1925, the coal hoists and their approach roads, originally laid by the Cardiff Railway, were subjected to a massive GWR improvement scheme, and the following selection of photographs shows the work that was carried out in the most difficult of circumstances. In the first, dated 24 February 1925, the base for a new concrete retaining wall is being prepared. To the left of this mess of mud, bricks and equipment, connected by the builders' temporary wooden walkways, can be seen high and low levels of the coal running lines. It is business as usual, even in this sea of chaos.

Elsewhere on the same day some track is laid and points are in position, with numerous piles of ballast ready for use. Shoring timbers have been secured in place to strengthen the higher-level curved embankments.

Above A month later, on 25 March 1925, the scene has changed around the existing tip roads towards the bottom of the south side of the dock. This scene shows the tightness of the curves that the trains of mineral wagons had to negotiate, without mishap, on their way towards the coaling appliances. In the foreground a GWR internal-user wagon and some others (probably for permanent way usage) are carrying spoil, and between them and the running lines sleepers are stacked ready for use.

Below Another view of the existing tip roads on the same day. Gas lamps are in use here, although electric lighting had been installed in the docks many years before, in 1888, but only in certain places. Next to the lamp is a point lever, usually operated by a shunter or a guard on a mineral train. In the distance are the luffing cranes, while on the gradient on the left is a rake of empty private-owner wagons, including one belonging to William Rowland & Co of Cardiff, then another belonging to W. H. Lever & Co, also of Cardiff.

Erecting coaling hoists near the inner lock gates of the Entrance Lock on 24/25 February 1925.

Above This is traverser hoist No 11, with a vessel coaling up alongside it on 25 February 1925; the hoist beyond is still under construction. Opposite, on the right, are weighbridge huts with a line of tall lamp posts between.

Below A private-owner seven-plank open wagon belonging to the Ocean Coal Company Ltd, Treorchy, is in its position on the cradle of one of the traverser hoists, and will soon be lifted and its contents deposited in the vessel's hold. The lifebelt hanging from the nearby pole is marked 'GWR A'.

Top On 25 February 1925 a solitary engine is taking water from a conical water tower, surrounded by the running lines to the hoists on one side, and the sea of mud and displaced track on the other. The design of the loco's forward-sloping side-tank assisted the driver's vision. The engine is probably one of the many built for the Cardiff Railway by Kitson & Co.

Middle On a misty 25 March 1925, a new concrete retaining wall is in position. On the extreme left is GWR Engineering Department three-plank open truck No 80382, behind which are lines of coal wagons from, among others, 'Bwllfa' (Bwllfa & Merthyr Dare Steam Collieries, at Aberdare), 'NN' (Nixon's Navigation Collieries at Mountain Ash and Merthyr Vale), 'BB' (Burnyeat, Brown & Co, owners of the Abergorki Colliery Nos 1, 2 and 3 pits, and the Tylacoch Colliery at Treorchy), and 'UN' (United National Collieries Co, owners of the Lady Margaret and Bute Pit at Treherbert, and other collieries at Wattstown and Risca).

Bottom Another general view on the same day shows another newly completed retaining wall. The internal-user wagons on the left seem to be carrying sleepers.

Above This elevated view, probably from the platform of a signal box, shows the running lines to Nos 6, 7, 8 and 9 coaling tips on the south side of Queen Alexandra Dock on 25 March 1925. In the distance is the silhouette of one of the power (or engine) houses that supplied hydraulic power to the quayside cranes. Between the semaphore signal and the power house is an engine on shunting duties, while long lines of empty and loaded wagons are everywhere.

Right Dated August 1925, this photograph is a bit of a mystery. Certainly a coal wagon is being hydraulically tilted upwards by use of the weighbridge hut's hydraulic ram. It may contain coal sludge, removed from the waters around the base of the coaling appliances and loaded into the wagon for tipping into this pit; this waste would then be removed by the buckets on the conveyor belt for use in the multi-heat furnace of the Crown Fuel Company, where it would be baked and pressed into moulds to be made into briquettes. Or it may simply be a wagon of household coal, and the conveyor belt system will enable the coal merchant to fill his 1cwt sacks and make his deliveries.

Storing of Welsh Coals and Fuels.

This is a very interesting subject, and in connection with same, I give the evidence issued in the Blue Book, Minutes of Evidence, Volume II, "Coal Supplies" (1903), by the late Sir Gordon Miller, Director of Navy Contracts, as follows :—

Q. "How long will Welsh Coal which is stored retain its properties ?"

A. "It is generally assumed that Welsh Coal will keep in good condition for twelve months under favourable circumstances. Experiments are about to be made to test the rate of deterioration for different periods at tropical depots."

Q. "I understand it will keep longer than that ?"

A. "I agree. Some places where it is necessary to store coal are in the tropics, where the climate is trying for coal, and that is one of the reasons why Welsh coal is so valuable, because it retains its properties under these circumstances.

Generally speaking, coals deteriorate after being stored for a length of time, but Welsh Steam Coals generally, and particularly the hard Black Vein Coals of Monmouthshire, are remarkable for their resistance to climatic influences either from heat or cold, and the latter show little or no deterioration after storage, and that principally of a physical nature. For use therefore in hot climates where storage is necessary, these coals are especially valuable.

The same remarks apply to Patent Fuel, which is exceedingly useful for storage, it being possible to build the briquettes into walls or cubes, another advantage being that any pilfering can then be at once detected.

The true Anthracite coals will bear storage for an indefinite period.

Weighing of Coals at Collieries and at Docks.

As regards the weighing of coals at the Colliery, I have little to say. The custom is that the coal should be weighed at the Colliery and afterwards at the Docks, but the weight at the Docks is the weight that can be absolutely relied upon. The coals are weighed upon machines which are carefully tested daily by an official of the Dock Company, known as Weighbridge Inspector, also at regular intervals by Government Inspectors. The coals are weighed in bulk, that is to say, the wagon containing the coal is weighed, and as the wagons contain on an average about ten tons, the quantities weighed are considerable. As the wagons proceed to the hoists, they pass over a weighbridge where the gross weight of wagon and coal is taken and recorded. Generally speaking, there are two railway lines leading to each hoist—one for loaded wagons, the other for empty wagons after they have been tipped. There is also a weighbridge on the railway line carrying the empties and all wagons are retared by the Dock Company free of charge. The retare weight of the empty wagon is deducted from the gross weight previously obtained, thus arriving at the net weight of coal shipped from the wagon. The weighing is open for everyone to see, and the weights are always open to inspection, so that they can be easily checked.

Above Storing conditions for Welsh coals and fuels, and the weighing procedures at collieries and docks, from a GWR Docks booklet, circa 1927.

Above In August 1925 a wagon's 7-ton load of coal is being hydraulically tipped into one of the 'Despatch'-type anti-breakage boxes, ready for one of the Lewis Hunter coaling cranes to lift the box into a vessel's hold and release the contents.

Left Another type of anti-breakage coal-loading box was the 'Jumbo', seen here circa 1922 with one of the men employed as a coal trimmer demonstrating just how large it is. It is seen here in its open position; the chains and brackets controlled the opening of the side doors. Coal trimmers were employed to spread the loaded coal around the ship's hold, thus keeping her on an even keel. These anti-breakage boxes helped to lessen the impact of the brittle Welsh coal landing in the hold, thus creating less dust than would otherwise be the case and spreading it around more.

Above In October 1935 vessels are 'bunkering up' with coal, ie taking on fuel for their own boilers, as well as for export. By this time Queen Alexandra Dock had movable coaling tips, which saved both labour and time, and could lift the new 20-ton coal wagons introduced under General Manager Sir Felix Pole and discharge coal at a rate of 800 tons per hour (see also page 126). The coaling tip's chute is clearly seen on the nearest vessel, directly in line with her hold.

Right In 1932 the *Great Western Railway Magazine* described 'new coal shipping appliances' at the docks: 'A new hoist with ancillary wagon traversing platforms, capable of shipping coal from 20-ton wagons, was brought into use at Cardiff Docks on 6 June 1932. The hoist completed a battery of five appliances of this description, which have been recently erected by the Great Western Railway at the Queen Alexandra Dock in pursuance of their policy of improving the coal shipping appliances at the docks under their control ... the hoists are of the latest type, and are fitted with the escalator type of anti-breakage appliances. Being movable, they enable coal to be shipped into any part of a vessel without the latter having to be moved in its berth. The hoists are worked by hydraulic power.'

This battery of nine of the new 20-ton coaling hoists, with traverser roads between, is seen in 1937. The hoists could be positioned so that more than one appliance could be used to load a vessel, which is what is happening here with the *Edmondo*. The second hoist has a Nixon's Navigation wagon on its traverser, which will soon be lifted; beyond, on the third hoist, is a 'GLM' wagon (Gueret Llewellyn & Marrett, whose wagons were built at the Cambrian Wagon Works, Cardiff, from English or American oak or of an all-steel construction). On the right the Nixon's Navigation wagon next to the weighbridge hut bears a different style of livery from that on the traverser. The warning sign 'Notice Beware of Moving Wagons' is repeated down the line of hoists; to its right two wooden wheelbarrows are being used to move a heap of dumped gravel, and the holes in the road, shown up by puddles of rainwater, will finally be filled in.

Above This photograph provides a good close-up view of the traverser in operation on a rather wet day in June 1947. On board the traverser is a 21-ton wagon, of all-steel construction, belonging to the GLM Company of Cardiff, No 91283. It carries a tare load of 10t 3cwt, and its centre panel reads 'Empty to Aberdare GWR'. The man beside the wagon is the traverser operator. Midway up the side of the hoist is the tip or chute operator, while the two men aboard the vessel are probably coal-trimmers, clearing any spilled coal from this vessel's deck and putting it back with the rest heaped up next to the funnel; some vessels carried extra ships' coal on top. Meanwhile, two members of the steamer's crew look on. Parked at the roadside is a Fordson motor car.

Left The traverser is now moving sideways to allow the tipped wagon, GLM No 122146, to access the returning track, seen alongside the full wagon. This is movable hoist or tip No 8, registered number 786, built in 1931 by The Hydraulic Engineering Co Ltd, of Chester.

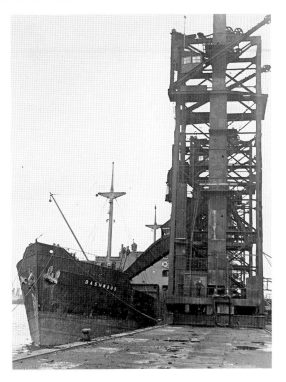

Above Also in June 1947 a loaded coal wagon, No 110024, is photographed during the tipping operation of a traverser hoist.

Above right This is a historical moment recorded on film: on 7 January 1948 the SS *Dashwood* is loading the first commercial cargo of Welsh coal to be shipped to France since the German occupation in 1940.

Below This photograph shows three paddle-steamers belonging to P. & A. Campbell's White Funnel fleet laid up for the winter in 1951. From right to left they are the *Glen Usk*, *Cardiff Queen* and *Bristol Queen*. The PS *Glen Usk* was built at Troon for Campbell's in 1914. She served her time during both World Wars as a minesweeper, and was sold for scrap in 1963; broken up at Cork, her steam whistle was put to good use at a brewery in Bristol.

Above Looking across the 'strongbacks' – the curved beams on the afterdecks of these two tugs – we can see a busy corner of the south side of Queen Alexandra Dock, circa 1966. A number of timber ships are berthed at Fletcher's Wharf, the new timber terminal. On the right is the *Welsh Herald* (port of registration Newport), and to the left is a vessel at berth alongside the cold store at King's Wharf. Note the mooring buoys marking the centre of the dock, while the cranes mark the area that is today's Coastal Containers Wharf.

Below In 1970 *Harbour Lights* magazine reported that 'The first nuclear submarine ever to visit Wales arrived at Cardiff on 6 April 1970. She is the HMS *Warspite* (1966, 3,500 standard displacement). Cardiff has also seen HMS *Manxman* (1941, 3,000sd), which arrived in early March, and HMS *Llandaff*

(1958, 2,170sd), which arrived in early May.' *Warspite* was seen entering the dock on page 22, and has now docked on the south side, which is a very different place from a decade before. Gone are the running roads to the coaling tips, and only rough grass and banks of earth mark where the coaling lines ran. The service road that marked the boundary between weighbridges and traverser hoists is still there, but nothing else. The mobile generators are charging the sub's batteries, the electric wires carefully held above the water by a float. Above the conning tower can be seen the submarine's snorkel (in the up position), and behind that is the bulbous shape of the radar dome (used for navigation and detecting an enemy's presence while on the surface). Behind the submarine is an abandoned ship's lifeboat, and in the left distance are the oil tanks of Curran Oils Ltd; to the right of the tanks is the pipework of the new Oil Berth.

Above This is the corner of the dock where the south side and King's Wharf meet, circa 1970. In the foreground is the tug *Tregarth* with another of the family behind, then two vessels at berth; the nearest is using her stern derrick to discharge part of her cargo. Over on the north side is the MV *S. A. Letara* of Cape Town, while tied up to the mooring buoys behind the *Tregarth* is the MV *Kings Reach*, of Glasgow.

Below The MV *Pötenitz* is discharging her cargo of deal at the quayside of the new Fletchers Wharf, Queen Alexandra Dock, circa 1970. She carries the Finnish style of ventilator tops.

Above On 23 April 2006 the *Fehn Sun* from St Johns, carrying a 2,800-tonne cargo of steel beams from Millazzo, is at the Duferco UK berth, with I Shed in view. Beyond the vessel is the Coastal Containers Wharf, with one of the company's ships at berth, being served by the container cranes. *Author*

Below Looking down the dock from King's Wharf, here is another view of the Coastal Containers Wharf. Very noticeable around the docks today is security fencing, some of which can be seen here, partly for health and safety reasons but mainly due to the International Ship & Ports Security Code, which came into force in July 2003. *Author*

2. RAIL ROUTES INTO THE DOCKS

An article in *The Railway Magazine* of 1908, describing the docks and their workings, informed readers that 'Cardiff, as all the world knows, is pre-eminently a coal port ... [but it] ... possesses many advantages for receiving imports.'

The article described all the railways that had direct access to Bute Docks, and explained that, in addition '...the Cardiff Railway collects and delivers goods by its own locomotives at all hours of the day and night from and to the junctions of the different railways, and thus furnishes means for the quick disposal of all traffic brought into or to be taken from the dock wharves and quays.

The import trade of the docks has more than doubled since the year 1880, and in 1907 the figure reached was 2,161,818 tons.'

Former Cardiff Railway 0-6-2T No 28, renumbered by the GWR as 159, built by Kitson & Co in 1887 to Works No 3069, is seen here at Cardiff Docks on 11 August 1924. It was sold to the NCB's Philadelphia Colliery in 1931 and renumbered again as No 55, and was scrapped in 1960. *LCGB, Ken Nunn Collection*

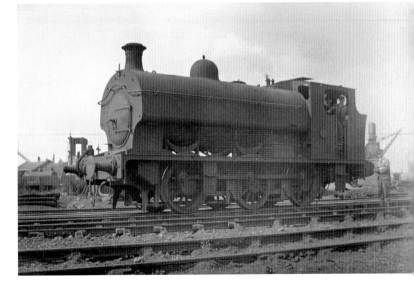

Cardiff Railway 0-6-0ST No 32 was photographed at Cardiff Docks on 10 September 1922, together with the driver and a guard on the footplate and the fireman on the ground. This loco was built in 1920 at Hudswell Clarke to Works No 1408, and was renumbered 684 by the GWR, which rebuilt it with a parallel boiler and pannier tanks in 1936. It was withdrawn from service in 1954. *LCGB, Ken Nunn Collection*

This 0-6-0 saddle tank, formerly Cardiff Railway No 19, is seen here on 7 August 1924, carrying its GWR number 697. Built in 1875 by the firm of Parfitt & Jenkins, it was fitted with a new boiler in 1921. Finally, at 50 years of age, it was withdrawn from service in 1925 and cut up for scrap in 1928. *RAS Publishing*

Taff Vale Railway

The Taff Vale Railway's West Branch Junction opened on 8 April 1840, but regular traffic only started running to the east side of Bute West Dock in June 1841; this branch closed in August 1964. The TVR's East Branch opened on 4 December 1848, with traffic going to the TVR's high-level tips; the rail connection from East Branch was taken out of use in 1953.

Below A TVR parcel label. *L. D. Bryant collection*

Below right From the Pontypridd Chronicle, 17 January 1885. *Pontypridd Library*

Right An Ordnance Survey map of 1920 showing the TVR line heading towards its Dock station terminus at Bute Street (left) and the East Branch Junction serving the east side of Bute West Dock and the west side of Bute East Dock (right). *Crown copyright*

Taff Vale Railway

TREHERBERT

TO

Cardiff Docks

THE AMALGAMATION OF THE TAFF VALE AND BUTE DOCK INTERESTS.

ACTION OF THE COAL TRADE.

A meeting of the coal trade was held at the Angel Hotel, Cardiff, on Wednesday, Mr. A. Hood presiding, and there also being present :—Messrs. Pratt, J. Cory, Thos. Evens, W. H. Lewis, W. Peere, L. Tylor, O. H. Riches, G. Bawn, A. Lusty, J. B. Ferrier, W. Simons (solicitor), and W. Gascoigne Dalziel (secretary). After a long discussion on the effect which the amalgamation of the interests of the Taff Vale Railway and the Bute Docks would have upon the trade of the district generally, it was resolved that the Bill to be introduced for the purpose of this amalgamation by the Bute Dock authorities be watched through Parliament, and, if necessary, the traders' interests be preserved by the insertion of protective clauses.

Left This photograph, taken on 31 March 1987, shows the abutments that once carried the by now long-disused TVR East Branch towards the Bute West and East Docks (see the map on the previous page). Class 37 No 37212 is running light towards Newport on the main South Wales line at 2.40pm, and a DMU from Queen Street is crossing on its way to Cardiff Central. *Author*

Below The Taff Vale Railway's code of whistles to be used by 'foreign' railways' engines when using the Bute Docks, 22 October 1894. *Author's collection*

APPENDIX OF WHISTLES ON FOREIGN RAILWAYS.

BUTE DOCKS COMPANY.

Stations and Junctions.	To and From	Whistles.	Remarks.
East Dock Junction and Maloney's Junction	High Level and Low Level	2 short	
	High Level and Maloney's	1 and 2 short	
	T.V.R. and Low Level	2 short and 1 crow	
	T.V.R. to Bute Railway	4 short	
	T.V.R. to Taff Vale Line	3 short	
	Up T.V. Line	1 short and 2 crows	
	T.V.R. and Reservoir Sidings	3 short and 1 crow	
	Reservoir Sidings and High Level	1 long	
	Reservoir Sidings and Taff Vale	1 and 1 crow	
	High Level and Reservoir Sidings	15 short	
	Bute Line Maloney's and T.V.R.	3 and 2 short	
	Bute Line Maloney's and High Level	3	
	Low Level and T.V.R.	2 and 4 short	
	Low Level and High Level	2	
East Dock Junction and Maloney's Junction	Bute Nos. 2 and 3 Maloney's Tips	2 crows	
	Bute No. 1 " "	3 crows	
	T.V.R. and Nos. 2 and 3 Maloney's Tips	2 short and 2 crows	
	" and No. 1 "	3 short and 2 crows	
	T.V.R. East Branch Main Line and Reservoir Junction	3 crows and 3 long	
	East Branch Sidings and Nos. 1, 2, and 3 Maloney's Tips	4 short and 1 crow	
	Nos. 2 and 3 Maloney's Tips and T.V.	1 and 4 short	
	Nos. 2 and 3 Maloney's Tips and Bute Line	2 and 2 short	
	No. 1 Maloney's Tip and T.V.R.	1 and 3 short	
	" " and Bute	2 and 3 short	
	Nos. 1, 2, and 3 Maloney's Tips and East Branch Sidings	1 crow and 4 short	
Roath Dock South-East and East Cabins	Blind Siding and T.V. Main	1 crow	
	South Side Roath Dock and T.V. Roath Branch	3 long	
	South Side Roath Dock and T.V. Empty Sidings	3 short and 1 long	
Roath Dock South-East and East Cabins	South Side Roath Dock and T.V. Main Line Storage	3 crows	
	No. 1 Tip Empty Road to Roath Branch T.V.	1 crow and 3 prolonged	
	No. 1 Empty Road and North Side Dock	1 crow and 1 long	
	Southernmost Wharf Road South Side and North Side of Dock	1 crow and 1 short	
	Southernmost Wharf Road South Side and Roath Branch	2 crows and 2 short	
	T.V.R. to No. 1 Down Line South Side	1 and 1 short	
	T.V.R. to No. 2 Down Line South Side	2 and 2 short	
	Full Storage and No. 1	2 short and 1 long	
	" and No. 2	2 short and 2 long	
	Main Line Storage and No. 1	2 long and 1 crow	
	" " and No. 2	1 crow and 2 prolonged	
	T.V. Storage and Blind Siding	2 crows	
	No. 1 Group of Empty Sidings and No. 1 Down Line	3 long and 1 short	
	No. 1 Group of Empty Sidings and No. 2 Down Line	3 long and 2 short	

BUTE DOCKS COMPANY (Con.)

Stations and Junctions.	To and From	Whistles.	Remarks.
Roath Dock South-East and East Cabins	No. 1 Group of Empty Sidings and Blind Siding	1 long and 2 short	
	No. 1 Group of Empty Sidings and Up Line	3 long and 3 short	
	No. 2 Group of Empty Sidings and Up Line	3 short and 1 long	
	Down Line and Blind Siding	1 crow	
	T.V.R. Storage and Up Main Line	3 crows	
	East and West on Up Main Line	1 long	
	Setting back on No. 2 Down Line	2 long and 2 short	
	Tip Roads and Up Line	2 long and 1 crow	
	" " No. 2 Down Line	3 long and 1 crow	
	" " No. 1 "	4 long and 1 crow	
	Up Road and No. 2 "	3 short	
	" " No. 1 "	4 short	
	Up Line and T.V.R. Branch	3 prolonged	
	Up Line and Blind Siding	1 long and 1 short	
	South Side to Machine and Wharf Roads	2 short and 1 crow	
	South Side Dock to Dowlais East Junction or Tharsis Works	3 short and 1 crow	
	Machine and No. 2 Down Line	2 short and 2 crows	
	Tharsis Copper Works and No. 1 Down Line	3 short and 2 crows	
	Tharsis Copper Works and No. 2 Down Line	2 crows and 3 short	
	Dowlais Works Eastern Junction and No. 1 Down Line	4 short and 2 crows	
	Dowlais Works Eastern Junction and No. 2 Down Line	2 crows and 4 short	
	No. 1 Down North and South Side Roath Dock	1 long	Up and Down Main Lines.
	No. 2 Down North and South Side Roath Dock	2 long	
	Shunt from No. 1 to No. 2 and vice versa	2 short	
	Shunt from No. 1 Down to Up Line and vice versa	4 short	
	Shunt from No. 2 Down to Up Line and vice versa	3 short	
	North—West Corner of Dock to No. 2 Down Line	2 long and 2 short	
	North Side Dock to South Side over No. 2 Down Line	2 long	

Great Western Railway, Bute Docks branch

The South Wales Railway opened its broad gauge branch on 17 January 1854. Just 1¼ miles long, it left the SWR main line at Long Dyke Junction.

The company amalgamated with the GWR on 1 August 1863, and by 1872 this broad gauge branch, together with other GWR lines, was converted to standard gauge. It was taken out of use briefly from July 2002 to October 2003, but is still in use as access to the docks via the Rod Mill Steelworks.

Above In this very informative photograph taken on 7 August 1961, looking north through the supports of the footbridge can be seen the dark shape of the Windsor Road overbridge, beyond which is Long Dyke Junction. The GWR Bute Docks line runs off to the left here at Tyndall Street Crossing (the signal box on the right), and the line in the foreground gives access to the north side of Roath Basin (see also the map overleaf). On the left, on the embankment, is a GWR signal box. *M. Hale*

Below An unused GWR wagon label, printed in April 1938. *A. G. Powell collection*

Below GWR No 683, formerly Cardiff Railway No 17, was built by Hudswell Clarke in 1920 to Works No 1407 as an 0-6-0 saddle tank, and was rebuilt as a pannier tank with a parallel boiler in 1926. It is seen here on 12 September 1951 while stopped alongside the wooden building of Edward & Snook, timber importers, of Tyndall Street. The crew are in the cab with the shunter on the ground with his trusty shunter's pole. Between engine and train is a GWR shunter's truck, complete with box containing the various items needed by the shunter, eg spare lamps, shunting poles, re-railing ramps, extra lamp oil, etc. It looks as though rain has diluted the cheap paint used on the timber merchant's building! No 683 was scrapped in 1954. *R. M. Casserley*

GREAT WESTERN RAILWAY
NON-COMMON USER WAGON
WHEN EMPTY RETURN TO:
G.W.R. TYNDALL STREET, JUNCTION

WAGON DUE AT JUNCTION

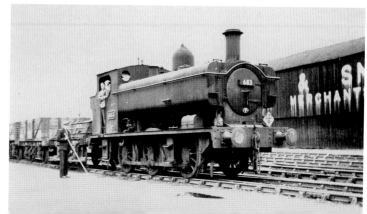

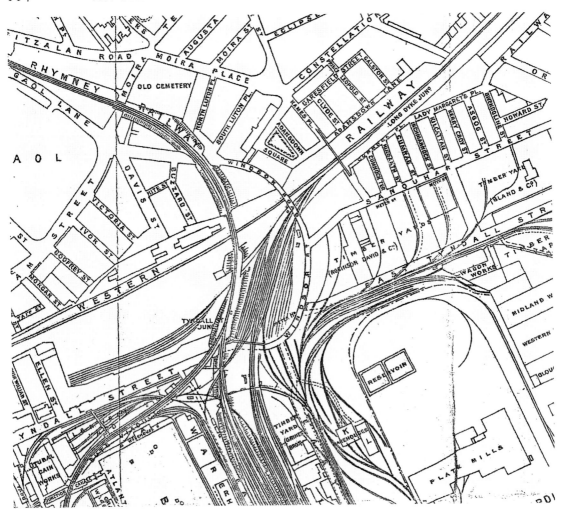

The photograph, taken on 19 June 1986 looking approximately south-east from the top left-hand corner of the 1913 OS map above, shows in the centre Windsor Road bridge and beyond it the timber yard of Robinson, David & Co, alongside Splott Road. The large building above the timber yard sheds was formerly the headquarters of the East Moors Steel Works. Bottom right is the former GWR goods depot, which by 1986 was the National Carriers Newtown Depot. Between the depot and the Windsor Road bridge can be seen the overgrown remains of the embankment that carried the Rhymney Railway's Bute Docks branch traffic south towards the docks. The GWR's Bute Dock branch (see previous page) passed beneath the furthest span of Windsor Road bridge.
Crown copyright/author

Rhymney Railway, Bute Docks branch

The Rhymney Railway's East Branch from the company's Adam Street station opened in December 1857, and was taken out of use on 20 December 1964. Running powers were granted to the LNWR.

Photographed from the end of the footbridge seen on page 113, 0-6-2T No 20 heads a coal train en route to the docks over Tyndall Street bridge, Cardiff, on 27 July 1922. Banking the train in the rear is another 0-6-2T, No 35. A few moments later the train will cross the bridge over the Junction Canal linking the Bute West and East Docks. *R. K. Cope, courtesy of R. S. Carpenter*

Tyndall Street signal box is seen on 3 May 1958, looking towards the docks. The former Cardiff Railway line curves away to the right to cross over the top end of the docks via the Bute Viaduct branch (which opened on 14 June 1859) to reach the west side of Bute East Dock; prior to the grouping this line would have been worked by Cardiff Railway engines and staff. The line to the left was the Rhymney Railway line, which took its engines to the Dock terminus, ie engine shed, and its coal wagons to the east side of Bute East Dock. The parapets of the two bridges seen a short distance south of the signal box both cross Tyndall Street. The chimneys on the extreme right belong to a Brains Brewery pub on Tyndall Street. In the vee of the junction is the square castellated building of the water works. *M. Hale*

This is the Junction Canal in November 1985, where it leaves Bute East Dock near Atlantic Wharf. It was once crossed by the railway, and this is what remains of the Bute Viaduct branch. Also looking very dilapidated on the left is the rear area of the former Spillers biscuit factory (see Volume 1). *Author*

Another view of the biscuit factory in November 1985, photographed from what is today known as Schooner Way; the curve of the rear wall matches the curvature of the nearby Bute Viaduct. The sign on the top of the building reads 'Spillers Bakers 1893'. A short distance from here, on the other side of the viaduct, was the LNWR goods station (see opposite). *Author*

London & North Western Railway

As mentioned above, the LNWR was granted running powers over the Rhymney Railway's lines as a reward for the company's financial help in the completion of the Rhymney's Caerphilly Tunnel, which enabled the RR to complete its new direct line into Cardiff, which opened on 1 April 1871. The LNWR began to use its new running powers four months later on 2 October 1871. As part of the London, Midland & Scottish Railway following the 'grouping' of 1923, it was decreed that these powers were to be discontinued on 1 January 1933, and instead LMS traffic would run over GWR lines using the route via Hereford and Newport to reach Cardiff Docks, and a short line to the company's Tyndall Street Goods Depot. This was reached by a half-mile connection from Tyndall Street Junction on the Rhymney Railway line, opened in 1875, the year in which the goods depot also opened.

Right A rear view of the LNWR's Tyndall Street Goods Depot, looking south. In the background can be seen the former Spillers biscuit factory (see opposite), both in a very sad state in November 1985. *Author*

Below This is the front of the goods depot, looking from the junction of the modern Schooner Way and Tyndall Street in September 1985. Schooner Way occupies the area where the wagon turntables were located in front of the loading bays (see the map overleaf). This grand old building is now listed. *Author*

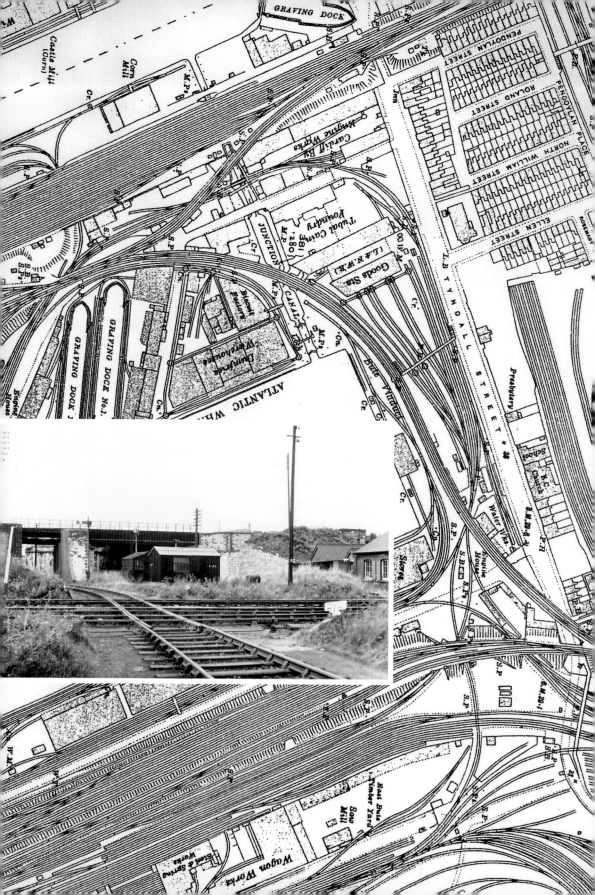

Opposite page The Ordnance Survey map of 1920 has been reproduced looking west, to correspond with the photograph, which shows the view from the bottom right-hand corner of the map on 7 May 1961. The line running left to right in the foreground is the former GWR Bute Docks line, heading left towards Roath Basin Junction and the north side of Roath Basin, and right towards Long Dyke Junction on the South Wales main line. The single line crossing them on the level is the former LNWR route, which then passes beneath the Rhymney Railway line (to the east side of East Dock), then the Bute Viaduct (carrying traffic to the west side of East Dock) before finally reaching the LNWR/LMS Tyndall Street Goods Depot, seen in the top centre of the map. Note to the left of the depot the Junction Canal and biscuit factory, behind the Dumfries Warehouses on **Atlantic Wharf.** *Crown Copyright/ M. Hale*

Top This photograph was taken on 7 March 1968 from the Rhymney Railway embankment looking down on the same scene as the photograph opposite. The single ex-LNWR line disappears from sight as it passes beneath this embankment towards the goods depot. In the distance, beyond the collection of huts, can be seen Tyndall Street footbridge, level crossing and signal box. *G. Morgan*

Middle One of the loading bays inside the goods depot in September 1985. *Author*

Bottom On 28 August 1988 this was the overall view of the area as seen from the high ground provided by the new Central Link road while still under construction. It shows the top end of East Dock; in the foreground is Tyndall Street, then the area of levelled ground that will eventually contain Howard Court, Keyes Court, Nelson Court and Atlantic Close, all built upon what was once goods yard and embankments. Two original buildings are being preserved and converted: on the left is the Spillers biscuit factory, and in the centre the former LNWR Goods Depot. *Author*

GWR branch from Pengam Sidings

Opened on 2 November 1903, this 1¼-mile long branch (with the Cardiff Railway company working a quarter-mile section) was scheduled to be taken out of use on 12 June 1978; however this was never implemented, and today this line carries the scrap steel much needed for the Celsa-owned Tremorfa Steelworks.

Above This is Pengam Sidings looking west, with the South Wales main line running to the right of the signal box. In the far distance is the former Taff Vale Railway bridge that carried TVR traffic over the GWR lines south towards Cardiff Docks. Former GWR 0-6-2T No 5636 takes a freight train from Cardiff Docks to join the main line at Pengam Junction on 24 January 1954. This '5600' Class engine was built at the GWR's Swindon Works in 1925, and withdrawn from service in 1962. *J. and J. Collection*

Below left Photographed from the same spot as the previous photograph, the Rover Way road bridge that crosses these busy lines, in June 1986 Class 37 No 37229 *The Cardiff Rod Mill* is hauling empty trucks via Pengam Junction back to the ASW Steelworks, or Tidal Sidings. On the extreme right is the former GWR Roath Goods Depot; the area beyond the building was once a coal and goods yard, but was cleared between 1984 and 1985. *Author*

Right An Ordnance Survey map of 1922 shows the GWR Roath Dock branch, starting from Pengam Junction on the South Wales main line (top centre). It then runs alongside the TVR Roath Branch, eventually crossing it, as the coal traffic of both companies heads southwards towards the numerous coal sidings built by the Bute Dock Company and capable of holding many hundreds of mineral wagons. *Crown copyright*

TVR Roath branch

This 5-mile branch, from Roath Branch Junction near Mynachdy on the outskirts of Cardiff, where sidings held a total of 2,240 wagons, opened on 24 August 1887, but it was not until 23 April 1888 that TVR traffic ran to Roath Dock. It was built under the provisions of the Taff Vale Railway Company Act of 1885, which dictated where 'railway No 1' (the Roath Branch proper) and 'railway No 2' (at the docks end) would commence from and where they would terminate at a junction near the Tharsis Copper Works. The double-track line ran through green fields

Right A 1970s map of the lower end of the TVR Roath Branch, showing Swansea Street Sidings, Marshalling Sidings and Tidal Sidings, and the Storage Sidings at Roath Dock.

and past garden allotments before reaching the TVR Roath Goods Depot and its sidings (renamed as Newport Road Sidings by the GWR in 1924). It then crossed the GWR South Wales main line and passed the Moorland Road biscuit works. Certain conditions had to be observed when the GWR main line was bridged; the TVR Act gave protection to the GWR in case of accidents while the TVR constructed the bridge of three spans, two of 58 feet and one of 48 feet long, over Newport Road and the GWR main line, and obliged the TVR to pay GWR men to act as lookouts. The branch closed on 6 May 1968.

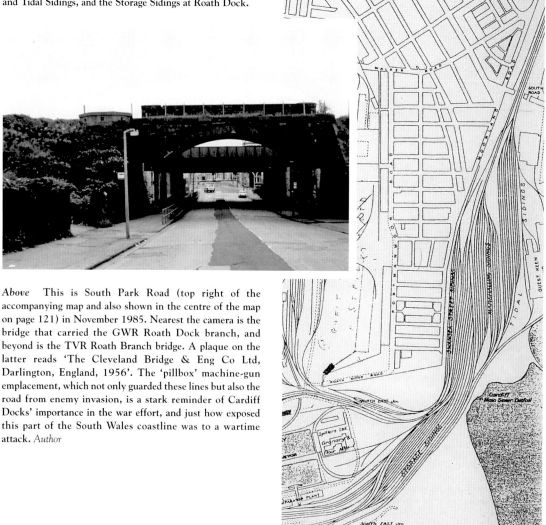

Above This is South Park Road (top right of the accompanying map and also shown in the centre of the map on page 121) in November 1985. Nearest the camera is the bridge that carried the GWR Roath Dock branch, and beyond is the TVR Roath Branch bridge. A plaque on the latter reads 'The Cleveland Bridge & Eng Co Ltd, Darlington, England, 1956'. The 'pillbox' machine-gun emplacement, which not only guarded these lines but also the road from enemy invasion, is a stark reminder of Cardiff Docks' importance in the war effort, and just how exposed this part of the South Wales coastline was to a wartime attack. *Author*

Above This is possibly Swansea Street Sidings, in August 1945. The war has ended, and the photograph shows eight tracks of government stores awaiting shipment overseas. To prevent pilfering certain items would be split into separate boxes when transported, eg left boots in one box, right boots in another.

THE MARITIME REVIEW. August 4, 1905

—THE—
Marquess of Bute's Collieries.

Shipping Agent:—
MR. SAMUEL JAMES,
1, Dock Chambers,
CARDIFF.

Telegraphic Address: "SEMA, CARDIFF.

"NIXON'S MERTHYR" Smokeless Steam Coal.

"FOTHERGILL'S ABERDARE" Smokeless Steam Coal.

"BUTE MERTHYR" Smokeless Steam Coal.

"DUFFRYN ABERDARE" Smokeless Steam Coal.

Nixon's Merthyr; and Fothergill's Aberdare; also Duffryn Aberdare Collieries are connected with the Taff Vale and Great Western Railway systems.

SHIPPING PORTS:

BUTE DOCKS, CARDIFF; PENARTH DOCK, SWANSEA, BRITON FERRY, and NEWPORT (MON.)

The Collieries are OLD-ESTABLISHED, and the qualities of the respective Coals are well-known in all the principal Markets.

Prices, F.O.B., or delivered into Buyers' Trucks.

Lewis Merthyr Consolidated Collieries, LIMITED.

Telegraphic Addresses:
"LEWIS MERTHYR, CARDIFF."
"LEWIS MERTHYR, LONDON."

OFFICES:

BUTE DOCKS, CARDIFF.

Secretary and Shipping Agent: W. H. JAMES.
London Agents: JAMIESON, GRIEVE & Co.
2, East India Avenue, E.C.
Liverpool Agents: R. & J. H. REA,
Old Castle Buildings.

Proprietors and Shippers of

"Lewis Merthyr" Navigation Steam Coal

Uniform in Quality, Highly Durable, Free from Spontaneous Combustion, and unsurpassed in Evaporative Power.

Used largely by the British, German, Italian and Dutch Governments, Cape Government Railways, by the following large Steamship Companies, viz.: Cunard, White Star, American Line, P. and O., Union Castle, Royal Mail, Orient, Pacific, Anchor Line, "Hansa" Line to India, Royal Hungarian Sea Navigation Company, "Adria" Limited, The Compagnie Generale Transatlantique, etc.

"LEWIS MERTHYR" is also extensively shipped to the principal Depots, Gibraltar, Malta, Port Said, Aden, Las Palmas, Cape De Verde, Grand Canary, etc.

OCEAN (MERTHYR) STEAM COAL.

PROPRIETORS:—

THE OCEAN COAL CO., LTD.,

—— 11, BUTE CRESCENT, CARDIFF.

OUTPUT.
UPWARDS OF TWO-AND-A-HALF MILLION TONS PER ANNUM.

This Coal is unrivalled for Steam Navigation and Railway purposes. It is well known in all the Markets of the World for

ECONOMY IN CONSUMPTION, ITS PURITY AND DURABILITY.

The Ocean Coal Company, Limited, have the largest unworked area of the celebrated Four Feet Seam of Coal in South Wales.

Right Advertisements from *The Maritime Review,* 4 August 1905.
Author's collection

Left Private-owner coal wagons at the Marshalling Sidings on the outskirts of Roath Dock in March 1927. All these wagons are en route to the coaling tips, with their end doors facing the camera. To the right are the Tidal Sidings. Visible are wagons from Nixon's Navigation Colliery (Abergorki Colliery) at Mountain Ash and Merthyr Vale (Nos 1 and 2); D. Davis & Sons, owner of the Ferndale Collieries in the Rhondda Fach; Burnyeat, Brown & Co ('BB'), owner of the Tylacoch Colliery and Abergorki Colliery, both near Treorchy; United National Collieries Co ('UN'); David Bevan & Co; and the Bwllfa Collieries at Bwllfa Dare, Aberdare.

Below Advertisements from about 1918. *Author's collection*

THE enormous coal traffic dealt with by the Taff Vale Railway entails railway generalship of no mean order. During the week ending December 1st, 1907, no less than 404,125 tons were conveyed over this railway. Including the return of empties, over 80,000 wagons within that period, equivalent to an average of nearly 14,000 a day, were conveyed over the 60 miles of line which constitutes the coal-carrying portion of the Taff Vale Railway. It is computed that 14,000 wagons standing on a railway would cover a distance of 24 miles of single line. This demonstrates the rapidity and exactness of working necessary to take within one day from colliery or dock siding, convey over miles of railway, and deliver at the receiving junctions or terminus this great amount of traffic. Such an achievement probably forms a record in respect to the volume of traffic transported over a similar length of line in the same working time, and reflects the highest credit on the general manager, Mr. A. Beasley, and his responsible officers.

Above The TVR's enormous coal traffic business is reported in *The Railway Magazine* in January 1908. The transportation of coal from colliery sidings to marshalling yards or docks was, on the whole, done with precision and the minimum of fuss. To move millions of tons each year might seem an impossible task, but with skill and planning it was done. Eight-ton wagons were used in the early days, then later 10-ton and 16-ton wagons became the norm. On average, a train leaving the Rhondda would take about 24 hours to reach the docks at Cardiff, owing to the congested railways during the boom years; the same applied on the return journey, with empties to be reloaded. However, waiting for empty wagons rarely stopped the collieries from producing coal; a never ending cycle had been created, and the owners caught the profits using a very large net – a 'net of opportunity'.

Right A GWR 'Weekly Summary of Wagons on Hand, Total Number Required and Forwarded' for Roath Sidings in July 1947. *Author's collection*

Below Coal awaiting shipment at Cardiff Docks, circa 1920.

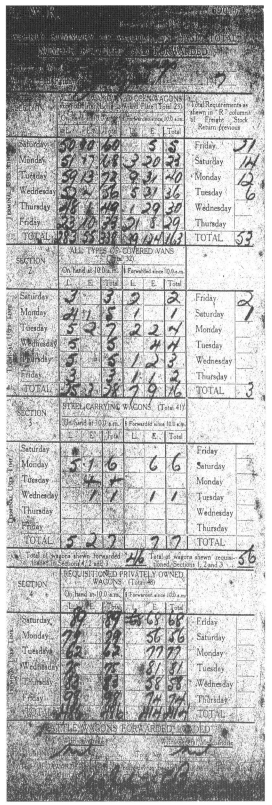

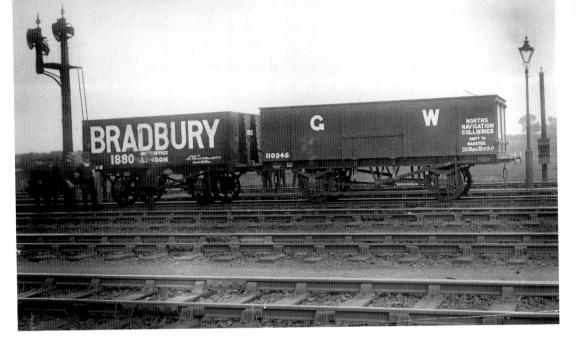

Above In the October 1924 edition of *The Railway Magazine* an article was published concerning the new GWR 20-ton coal wagons:

In September of last year, a letter was issued under the signature of Sir Felix J. C. Pole, General Manager, Great Western Railway, inviting coal owners in areas served by the Great Western Railway, and particularly in South Wales, to use 20-ton instead of 10- or 12-ton wagons. As an inducement they were offered a rebate of 5% off the railway company's rates in respect of coal class traffic conveyed wholly over the Great Western system in fully loaded 20-ton wagons. Since then, negotiations have been proceeding between the railway company and the traders for the adoption of the 20-ton wagons, but in some quarters it was apparently felt that it would not be practicable to give effect to the change. These fears are, however, disappearing, and the first complete train of 20-ton wagons arrived recently in the South Wales area. The train, consisting of 50 all-metal wagons affording a maximum capacity of 1,000 tons, created very keen interest in its passage down the line en route for Messrs

North's Navigation Collieries, Maesteg. It proved to be the forerunner of 30 such trains, which will work into South Wales during the next two or three months for the use of various traders, an achievement which in so short a time represents notable progress in the evolution of coal transport in South Wales. The firms who have already availed themselves of the advantages of the scheme are North's Navigation Collieries Ltd, D. R. Llewellyn, Merrett & Price, Bedwas Navigation Colliery Co Ltd and Crumlin Valley Collieries Ltd. Other firms that are closely considering the matter are Bradbury, Son & Co Ltd, Stephenson, Clarke & Co Ltd, Tredegar Iron & Coal Co Ltd, United National Collieries Ltd, and the Ebbw Vale Steel, Iron & Coal Co Ltd.

The photograph compares an older 12-ton and a modern 20-ton wagon.

Below After its naming ceremony on 23 May 1984, No 37229 *The Cardiff Rod Mill* stands waiting to haul 1,000 tons of steel from the Tidal Sidings. *BR*

Above This was the view from the former Marshalling Sidings area at the end of Splott Road in September 1984, showing a varied selection of British Rail wagons, tankers and hoppers waiting on the Tidal Sidings. Behind is the ASW Steelworks, on the closure of which the Tidal Sidings were to be taken out of use on 31 July 2002; however, this was never implemented due to negotiations leading to the re-opening of the Tremorfa Steelworks, purchased by the Celsa Steel group on 1 July 2003. *Author*

Right A BR Train List (under the TOPS system of wagon control), dated 24 August 1987, issued at Radyr Depot and listing mineral train movements from Tidal Sidings to Aberthaw Power Station. Today railway traffic enters Cardiff Docks via Long Dyke Junction, passing beneath Windsor Road and following the former GWR route towards the Castle Works Steelworks and the Tremorfa Steelworks. English Welsh & Scottish Railway (EWS) traffic also enters the docks via Pengam Junction, Cardiff, passing beneath Rover Way and following the former GWR route towards Tidal Sidings, before continuing towards the south side of Roath Dock. *A. G. Powell*

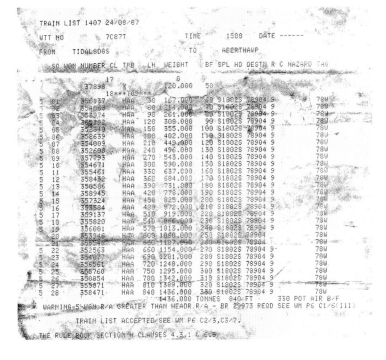

3. THE ENTRANCE CHANNEL

The port of Cardiff is situated under the high ground of Penarth Head, being well sheltered from westerly winds. However, because of the natural geological conditions of the Bristol Channel, aided by the flowing waters of the Taff, Ely and Rhymney rivers, a vast amount of muddy silt is carried in suspension by the tidal waters of the Channel, and tends to settle here, forming huge mud banks and areas of shallow water. To provide a suitable depth of deep water for vessels using the approach channel en route to Cardiff Docks, a regular amount of dredging takes place to provide a depth of between 39ft 3in at high water on a spring tide and 29ft 9in at high water on a neap tide. During the 1920s, for example, 30,000 tons of mud was dredged each week from this Entrance Channel alone.

In the 1960s a scheme was put forward by the Cardiff Pilots suggesting a deep-water harbour about a mile and a half down-channel from the present Queen Alexandra Dock, in the vicinity of Penarth Pier, but this was not implemented. This was presumably as a result of continuing problems with ships running aground. Late in 1969 *Ship Ahoy* magazine reported that the *Pollinia*, an ore carrier (1962, 17,298gt) had run aground off Penarth while bound for Cardiff on 9 November; fortunately she came off on the same tide, but had to return to Barry as the tide was on the ebb. Likewise, on 18 October the *Texaco Gloucester* (1959, 12,834gt) was grounded in the wrack channel off Penarth Pier while on a voyage from Milford Haven to Cardiff with 16,000 tons of fuel oil. Attempts to refloat her on the following tide failed, but on the midday tide of 19 October six Rae tugs successfully refloated her, after some 1,000 tons of cargo had been transferred to two local Harker tankers. Happily, the *Texaco Gloucester* was not damaged.

When the 'Sea Canal' (later known as Bute West Dock) was about to be constructed, the Marquis of Bute excavated an area that had been scoured out by the reaction of the sea water mixing with the flow of fresh water from the River Taff. This formed a natural basin close to the entrance of the dock, and later became known as the Tidal Basin or Steam Packet Harbour.

A Low Water Pier for passenger ships crossing the Bristol Channel was opened on 16 September 1868 to coincide with the coming of age of the 3rd Marquis of Bute. Two years later a passenger station was built on the pier, and a passenger railway service started on 8 July 1870, running from the Rhymney Railway's Parade station to the pier. These cross-channel passenger services were advertised by the Rhymney Railway on its railway notice boards as well as being mentioned inside its timetable booklets. Constructed of wood, the pier was 1,400 feet long and 34 feet wide, was provided with a railway and a carriageway, and was also equipped with a floating pontoon, a vertical hydraulic lift and a 10-ton crane. In 1900 the Low Water Pier pontoon was transferred to a new position alongside No 1 pontoon, and became No 2 pontoon. The pier was never rebuilt after being destroyed by fire in 1919.

Heading north up the Entrance Channel towards the Bute Docks, in the early years of the 20th century we would have seen on our right the newly finished embankment that would eventually provide the boundary for the proposed new South Dock, later to become known as the Queen Alexandra Dock. Then we would see the now disused Low Water Pier, marked on maps as 'Old Pier' and 'Old station', describing the area once used by passengers embarking on cross-channel trips. A lighthouse was situated alongside, at the southernmost point of the pier, after which was the entrance to a dry dock, alongside which was a landing stage and pontoon on the seaward side of its buildings. After passing this pontoon there were coaling staithes and, beyond them, mooring posts known as dolphins.

Above A faded but historic view of the Entrance Channel from the Pierhead, taken at 5.30pm on 23 May 1884, at high water. Dredgers are working on the right, with steam tugboats bunched together on the left. In the centre a steam tug is bringing in a sailing vessel, and the 'C' on the sail of the boat nearby indicates that it is a Cardiff-based Pilot cutter, responsible for safe entry into the docks, especially as the vessel is now in the hands of the Pilot.

Right This photograph is quite unique, as it gives a view of the Low Water Pier, some 16 years after its opening, photographed at 7.30pm on 23 May 1884. The pier carried a railway station, lighthouse and flag post at the far end. Across the water is Penarth Head and St Augustine's Church, silhouetted against the skyline. The dredgers are seen again on the right in more detail; they are a pair of bow-well, non-self-propelled, bucket ladder dredgers (also known as bucket dredgers), which were moved about by tugs. The silt and mud was transferred via a chute into hopper barges that came alongside and took the spoil out to sea.

Right This third view from the Pierhead was taken at 1.00pm on 26 May 1884, 3 hours before high tide, hence the mud banks visible on the right. In the centre are the bucket dredgers with a hopper barge on the right and a steam tug on the left.

Next we would see the lock gates of Roath Basin, then, between those gates and the lock gates of East Dock Basin, the Gridiron. Constructed by the Bute Docks Company, this consisted of large baulks of timber laid horizontally, upon which was laid the keel of a ship, and wooden staging on the shore side, against which the ship was supported; the vessel, having taken up its position on a falling tide, would be left high and dry as the water receded. The Gridiron measured 350 feet long by 35ft 9in wide (later reduced by 9 inches).

Now heading west for a short distance, we pass by the front of the dock offices, with its magnificent red brickwork, and the Bute West Basin lock gates, before turning southwards again down the other shoreline, and into the Tidal Basin. This was the site of the old Tidal Harbour, which was 1,000 feet long by 500 feet wide and covered 11 acres, at a depth of 36 feet at high water. There were 12 large hydraulically operated coaling tips here on the north and west sides. Here also were the two landing stages used by P. & A. Campbell's paddle-steamers, behind which were general offices, a cargo warehouse, and the Pilotage Office.

The following extract is from the Bute Docks (Cardiff) Bye-Laws and Regulations, 1886 and 1887, issued by William Thomas Lewis, General Manager:

Pilot boats, tug boats, and other craft must not be allowed to lie or remain in the Steam Packet Harbour, or in the course of the traffic to these docks. Vessels bound into the Bute Docks shall, after rounding the fairway buoy, take up a position on the east side of mid channel, at least a cable's length astern of preceding vessels, which distance must be maintained. Vessels bound from the Bute Docks to sea must keep to the westward of the channel, and maintain at least a cable's length distance from the vessel ahead, and pass out to sea through the entrance channel, so that the rule of port helm must be always applied to clear vessels both outwards and inwards.

The amalgamation of the Barry, Cardiff and Newport pilotage authorities and services was proposed at the end of 1970, with an anticipated reduction in the number of pilot cutters in service.

After passing the landing stages we see the premises of the Mountstuart Shipbuilding Yard, comprising two docks marked on the map of 1901 as Graving Dock No 1 and No 2, with a pumping house located on the left of the caisson gates.

Comparing the foregoing with the OS map of 1922 (page 10), certain changes have taken place. Most noticeable is that the Entrance Channel has been greatly widened as it now includes the outstretched arms of the Queen Alexandra Dock entrance. Also, the Mountstuart Shipbuilding Yard now has three Graving Docks, two long and thin with a shorter, fatter one between, after which at the southernmost tip is a landing stage.

The following extract from the Bute Docks (Cardiff) Bye-Laws and Regulations of 1886 and 1887 describes the signals applicable to the Steam Packet Harbour and Entrance Channel:

An ordinary signal post and arm is erected for each berth at the pontoons, Nos 1 and 2 in the Steam Packet Harbour. The signal post for the berth at the south side of No 2 pontoon is raised to the height of 10 feet above the top of the dolphin, the signal post for the berth at the north side of No 2 pontoon is raised 15 feet above the top of the dolphin, the signal post for the berth at the south side of No 1 pontoon is raised to the height of 20 feet above the top of the jetty, and the signal post for the berth at the north side of No 1 pontoon is raised 25 feet above the top of the jetty.

When any berth is blocked against the approach of a vessel, the signal arm for such berth will remain in a horizontal position, and the lowering of the arm will signify that the vessel may approach the pontoon.

Red and green discs are affixed to the arms of the signal posts, and from sunset to sunrise the signal that a berth is blocked will be a red light and the signal that it is available will be a green light.

No vessel shall come alongside or endeavour to attempt to come alongside a berth until the signal is given that the berth is available.

Right An extract from the Taff Vale Railway timetable for July, August and September 1892, showing Channel sailings from Cardiff. *Author's collection*

CHANNEL SAILINGS FROM CARDIFF.

CARDIFF and WESTON.—This service is a daily one (Sundays excepted) of several trips. Cheap through fares are in operation from Taff Vale Railway Stations, as shown on page 23.

CARDIFF and ILFRACOMBE.—A service is run between these places on four or five days a week by the "Bonnie Doon" or other steamer. For times see Bristol Channel Passenger Service bills. Through tickets are issued from Taff Vale Railway Stations, as shown on page 23.

On special days cheap daily return tickets are issued from Cardiff to Lynmouth and Ilfracombe. Weekly and two monthly tickets are also issued from Taff Vale Stations to Ilfracombe. Particulars may be obtained at the Booking Offices and of the Steamboat Agents, Messrs. Edwards, Robertson & Co., Bute Docks, Cardiff.

THROUGH BOOKINGS TO STATIONS ON LONDON & SOUTH WESTERN RAILWAYS.—Single and return tickets, are issued at Taff Vale Railway Stations to Stations on the London and South Western Railways, *via* Cardiff and Ilfracombe Steamboat Service. Holders of single tickets must complete their journey on the day following date of issue. Return tickets are available on the forward journey as above, and on the return journey any day while the service of steamboats continues to run, not exceeding one month after date of issue. See Table of fares on page 22.

NOTE.—The Steamboat Season will end about September 15th.

NOTICE.—Through Tickets, available by these steamboats, are issued by the Taff Vale Railway Company on condition that they are not to be held liable for any injury, damage, loss or detention whatever which may occur to passengers or their luggage during, or in respect of, the journey by steamboat.

The fares shown on pages 22 and 23 do not include conveyance between the railway and steamboat, or exempt passengers from the payment of pier dues.

Below right The Bute Docks (Cardiff) Bye-Laws and Regulations, 1886 and 1887, described the flags to be flown on the Low Water Pier during the daytime, and the position and colours of the lamps at night, as follows:

The following Signals are exhibited at the Low Water Pier:
When there is a free stem for all docks, a black ball at the head of the eastern signal staff.
When there is a free stem for the West Dock, a black ball on the western signal staff.
When there is a free stem for the East Dock, a black ball at the western yard of the eastern signal staff.
When there is a free stem for the Roath Dock, a black ball at the eastern yard of the eastern signal staff indicates that vessels may come ahead.
When there is a stemming list, a red flag with white St Andrew's cross placed
    for the West Dock, on the western signal staff
    for the East Dock, on the western yard of the eastern signal staff
    for the Roath Dock, on the eastern yard of the eastern signal staff
indicates that vessels on the list may come ahead.
A blue flag at the masthead indicates that all docks are closed for the tide.
A blue flag on the western signal staff indicates that the West Dock is closed.
A blue flag at the western yard of the eastern signal staff indicates that the East Dock is closed.
A blue flag on the eastern yard of the eastern signal staff indicates that the Roath Dock is closed.
A red light indicates that vessels on the list for West Dock may come ahead.

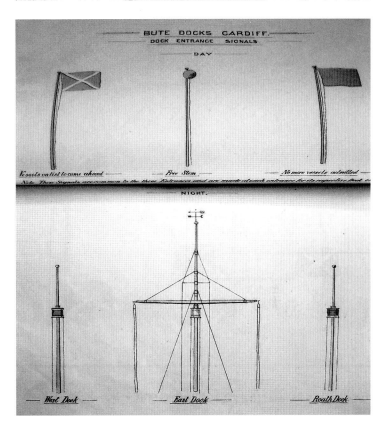

A green light indicates that vessels on the list for West Dock may come ahead, and a white light indicates that vessels on the list for East Dock may come ahead.
When the blue flag is exhibited, any vessel, even on the list for entering the docks and approaching the same, must at once stop and turn back to her lying ground in the roads.

Above In June 1949 the old signal mast is being dismantled with the help of the floating crane and two steam tugs, while on the left is a new temporary one. At its base is another wartime brick and concrete pillbox, and in the far distance is Penarth Pier.

Below At the top of the Entrance Channel is the Tidal Harbour area, seen here with the West Dock Basin entrance beyond, and the light/signal tower that provided a visual aid for and controlled the movement of vessels into the docks. The steps built into the sea wall provided access to the small boats moored below; a steam tugboat is moored against the wall at the extreme left. Over on the extreme right is the East Basin entrance, with a coaling appliance and the Hydraulic Power Station. This hand-coloured postcard is postmarked and dated Cardiff No 3, 5.30pm, 13 July 1907, the day that King Edward VII and Queen Alexandra declared the Queen Alexandra Dock open. The short message is to Miss Alexander of Ystrad House, Hill St, Newport, Mon, and reads '10.30am. I am down here waiting to see the King. Left home at 8.25. Quite well.' *Author's collection*

Above This circa 1905 postcard again shows the West Dock Basin entrance, this time with a small coaster leaving the dock, and one of the Cardiff-based Pilot Cutter boats waiting for what looks like a fishing vessel to pass by, before escorting the coaster down the Entrance Channel. On the sail of the cutter is a large 'C' and a small 'F', identifying its home port. These boats also carried a fleet number and name, usually at the bow, and were approximately 45 feet in length. Above the large sail they would fly the white over red colours of their flag of office. *G. G. Jones collection*

Right This postcard shows a Cardiff Pilot Cutter at Hillsboro, near Ilfracombe, which illustrates just how far these boats travelled in the line of duty. *L. D. Bryant collection*

This photograph shows a mix of steam and sail. In the background, on the extreme left, is Bute Crescent and the distinctive Powell Duffryn Colliery Company building, and, to its right, the Mission for Seamen Church, then the Pierhead Building of the Cardiff Dock Company, with the West Dock and East Dock entrances on either side. Then can be seen the Gridiron sloping down towards the water's edge, to the right of which is the Customs Boarding Station. Further right again are the chimney and buildings of the Hydraulic Power House. The date is about 1900, and No 2 pontoon, after its removal from the Low Water Pier, is being repositioned to be moored alongside the Gridiron with the assistance of at least three steam tugs. The rowing boat in the foreground is carrying the boatmen who would 'take' (carry) the ropes between vessels or the shore as requested.

A Port of Cardiff Pilot's Report, dated 13 December 1869. *L. D. Bryant collection*

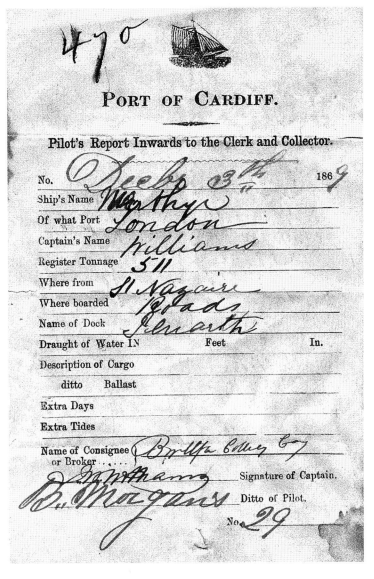

PORT OF CARDIFF.

Pilot's Report Inwards to the Clerk and Collector.

No. *Decbr 23th* 186*9*

Ship's Name *Merthyr*

Of what Port *London*

Captain's Name *Williams*

Register Tonnage *511*

Where from *St Nazaire*

Where boarded *Roads*

Name of Dock *Penarth*

Draught of Water IN Feet In.

Description of Cargo

ditto Ballast

Extra Days

Extra Tides

Name of Consignee or Broker ..... *Bryllffa Colliery Coy*

Williams — Signature of Captain.

W. Morgans Ditto of Pilot.

No. *29*

This is the office building of the South East Wales Pilotage Authority, which was located in Stuart Street, adjacent to the entrance to the Mountstuart Dry Docks, photographed in June 1984. The Cardiff Pilotage Board was established under the Bristol Channel Pilotage Act of 1860, and has since been absorbed into Docks Authority control. *Author*

4. THE MOUNTSTUART DRY DOCKS

In 1882 the Mount Stuart Shipbuilding Graving Docks & Engineering Company Ltd acquired a shipyard to the south of the Packet Harbour, together with a dry dock; a second dry dock was opened alongside in 1884. The term 'graving' means cleaning a boat's bottom.

The Docks & Harbour Authority booklet of May 1957 stated that the firm was then known as the Mountstuart Dry Docks Ltd, and that the yard consisted of three dry docks: No 1 had an initial length of 440 feet with a width of 52ft 3in, later altered to 420 feet by 52 feet, and finally extended to 430 feet by 52ft 9in; No 2 was initially 420 feet long by 52 feet wide, then became 400 by 52 feet,

and was finally extended to 495 feet long by 63 feet wide; No 3 was initially 550 feet long by 66 feet wide, then became 565 by 66 feet, and a final extension made it 543 feet in length by 66 feet wide.

Ship Ahoy magazine, in the summer of 1962, announced that a development for the benefit of ship-owners had recently been introduced by the Mountstuart Dry Docks, in conjunction with Treharne & Davies, the Cardiff firm of industrial analysts and consultants. They offered the services of a mobile laboratory, with more than £3,000 worth of instruments, which was available day and night to be taken alongside ships to provide facilities for important tests relative to shipping problems.

Both the Channel Dry Dock and the Mountstuart Dry Docks were affected by the construction of the Cardiff Bay Tidal Barrage, and subsequently became part of the Cardiff Bay development scheme.

STILL, the Channel Dry Docks isn't the only pebble on the shiprepairing beach, if you'll forgive us for placing the matter in that somewhat poetical manner. There is the Mountstuart Dry Docks, for example. Keeping to the metaphorical idea, it is a fairly good sort of pebble, don't forget. Jealous folk are apt to say things up against the Mountstuart Dry Docks—especially when dividends are the subject of discussion. But that is merely human, isn't it? If you were managing a dry dock which never—even in the "boom"—paid more than three per cent., and at the same time had to consider a dry dock which paid ten per cent., and a 2½ per cent. bonus—well, you'd get wrathy, and would say things, wouldn't you? Of course, you would—unless you were a sort of double-breasted Christian, in which case, you might find a difficulty in squaring matters—but never mind!

+ + +

BUT reverting to "the Mountstuart," which has paid out that "ten and two-and-a-half," more'n once, yes—well, it's no wonder that the three-per-cents. say things up against it? Never mind ; just you read the following : "The directors' report for the year ended June 30, showed a profit, after paying interest on the debentures, of £21,169. After providing for the interim dividend, and a further distribution at the rate of six per cent. per annum on the preferred, and four per cent. per annum on the deferred shares . . . a balance remained of £4,518 to carry forward." Very well then. The foregoing is an excerpt from the directors' report of the Mountstuart Dry Docks, Limited. It's good enough—alongside of the old three-per-cent., isn't it? Certainly!

Left The Mountstuart Dry Docks' success compared with others: an extract from *The Maritime Review*, 4 August 1905. *Author's collection*

Right A 1920 Ordnance Survey map showing the location of the 'Mountstuart Shipbuilding Yard' and its three Graving Docks. Next to the docks are the Pontoon Landing Stages Nos 1 and 2, belonging to P. & A. Campbell Ltd and used by their paddle-steamers; No 1 was in place by 1860, and No 2 came from the Low Water Pier in 1900 (see page 134). A single railway line serves the area: passing down the west side of Bute West Basin, it passes the Mission for Seamen Church and the Merchants' Exchange before crossing the road at the junction of Bute Street and Stuart Street, to thread its way between the Pilotage Office and a cargo warehouse, before branching to serve the cluster of landing stages and graving docks. *Crown Copyright*

Inset A 15-ton electric crane, fitted with a horizontal luff, in use at the Mountstuart Dry Docks, circa 1922.

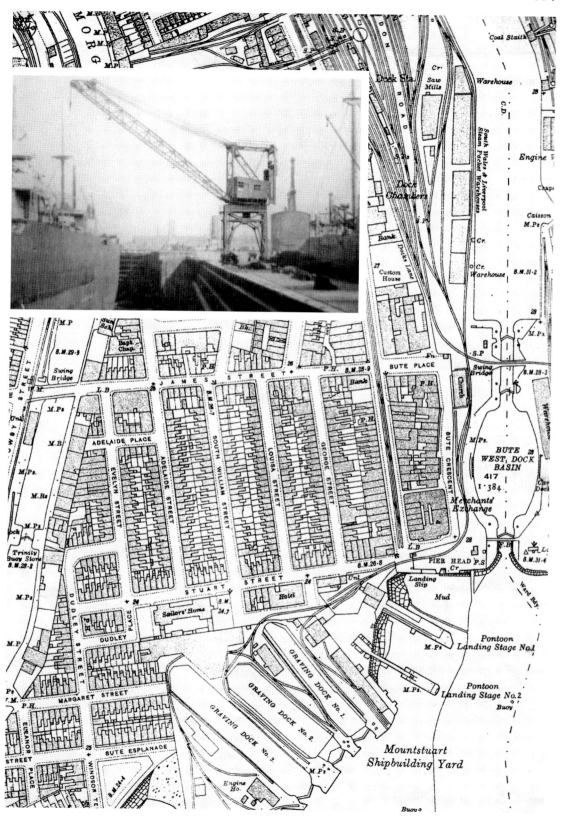

Left The Scarweather Light Vessel in Mountstuart Dry Dock in the spring of 1966. *C. Collard*

Above The paddle-steamer *Westward Ho* is moored at the landing jetty, providing a good side view of the Mountstuart Dry Docks, again in the spring of 1966. On 24 June of that year the 60-year-old Cardiff Pontoon No 2 sank shortly after 150 schoolchildren had boarded the *Westward Ho*. Divers found an 18-inch hole in the pontoon's bottom, and repairs were completed by 26 June; in the meanwhile Penarth was used as a substitute port, with the up-channel boats going to Barry at night. *C. Collard*

Below This is the view from the Pierhead on 29 April 1987, looking across the Tidal Harbour towards the entrance passages to the graving docks and the buildings that were once connected with the Mountstuart Dry Docks. *Author*

5. P. & A. CAMPBELL'S PADDLE-STEAMERS

No work on Cardiff Docks would be complete without a mention of the firm of Messrs P. & A. Campbell, whose White Funnel fleet of paddle-steamers were a familiar sight for many people over the years.

The development of the White Funnel fleet of paddle-steamers belonging to brothers Paul and Alec Campbell started in the Bristol Channel in 1888. They had recognised the importance of the area, and the need for cross-channel excursion services operating from Cardiff to Barry, Bristol, Ilfracombe, Newport and Weston-super-Mare, so they sold their steamboat business on the Firth of Clyde to their competitor, the Caledonian Steam Packet Company, and moved to the tidal bay area of the Port of Cardiff. The brothers had made a

Right This postcard view from about 1910 shows the ticket office and reception area for customers wishing to sail on one of P. & A. Campbell's paddle-steamers. In the centre is the gangway for passengers to board their vessel, and on the right one of the paddle-steamers, the *Ravenswood*, has docked at the pontoon. Once its passengers are ashore immediate preparations will be made to receive the next group. Behind the *Ravenwood* can be glimpsed another paddle-steamer, the *Britannia*. *G. G. Jones collection*

Below One of the White Funnel fleet, believed to be PS *Britannia*, is seen in this postcard view from about 1920. She returned from war service in 1919, and had changes made to the window arrangement and to her upper structure in 1921. She is seen here in the Tidal Harbour, and to the left is one of the landing stages used by the paddle-steamers. *Author's collection*

P. & A. CAMPBELL Limited.

WHITE FUNNEL FLEET

Sailings from CARDIFF & PENARTH by Saloon Steamers of the

Britannia, Cambria, Devonia, Glen Avon, Westward Ho, Waverley, Glen Usk, Glen Avon, &c.

Timetable of White Funnel Fleet sailings from Cardiff and Penarth, circa 1934. A. G. Powell collection

Dominant in this photograph is the house flag of the Docks & Inland Waterways Executive, circa 1950. Behind the flag is the passenger pontoon and access gangway, with two P. & A. Campbell paddle-steamers at berth; eventually this pontoon had to be taken out of service for safety reasons. The paddle steamer with two funnels is the *Cardiff Queen*, and the other is the *Ravenswood*. Beyond them can be seen a vessel in the Mountstuart Dry Docks. Two wooden 'dolphins' are also in view, which once held semaphore signals informing vessels when it was safe to enter these pontoon berths; the one just behind the paddle-steamers shows a round ring on the arm, indicating 'not in use'. This photograph also gives a good indication of the Bristol Channel tidal range, and shows just how important it was to keep the Entrance Channel clear of mud for shipping moving in and out of the docks.

wise and soon to be profitable decision, for the paddle-steamers of P. & A. Campbell dominated the coastal cruising and ferry operations for 80 years. For a while their field of operation even included the South Coast of England.

However, by the 1950s a decline in the excursion trade was causing problems, and with costs spiralling it was the beginning of the end for this well-established but outdated firm. Vessels were laid up in the hope of a revival miracle, but at the end of 1959 the company passed into the hands of the receiver. Yet hope wears many disguises, and on 31 December 1959 the remains of the fleet became part of George Nott Industries, part of the Townsend Ferries group, albeit with only two paddle-steamers and one laid up. The former boom days would not return, but at least P. & A. Campbell and its paddle-steamers were back in business for a few more years. Sadly, in the early part of 1981 the company's cross-channel operation finally ceased.

Westland hovercraft SRN2, belonging to P. & A. Campbell, leaves the Queen Alexandra Dock Entrance Lock on 22 July 1963. No 001, weighing 27 tons, had arrived at Cardiff the previous day via the *Bay Fisher*, and on the 22nd it carried a 42-strong party of VIPs, including the press, on trips from Penarth. The service between Penarth and Weston was officially inaugurated on the 23rd, with six crossings daily Monday to Friday in both directions.

ORDNANCE SURVEY REFERENCES

The following National Grid references cover the main locations around Queen Alexandra Dock.

Queen Alexandra Dock

Entrance lock, outer to inner gates	ST1977533-ST196735
North side (to Bell's Wharf)	ST195734-ST199741
Empire Wharf	ST201742-ST201744
King's Wharf	ST201742-ST202741
South side	ST197735-ST202741
Pit prop storage area	ST203745-ST205747
Beach Sidings	ST203738-ST207743
Roath storage sidings	ST208752-ST209754
Swansea storage sidings	ST208755-ST206759
Marshalling sidings	ST209757-ST206763
Tidal sidings	ST209756-ST206764

ACKNOWLEDGEMENTS

I would like to thank the following for their help with these books:

Dr Don Anderson, Roath, Cardiff (former editor of *Ship Ahoy* magazine); Associated British Ports, Cardiff; Birmingham Central Library; Ian Bolton, Social Sciences Department, Birmingham Central Library; Brenda Brownjohn, *The Railway Magazine*, London; L. D. Bryant, Pencoed, Mid Glamorgan; Sarah Canham, Research Centre Assistant, National Railway Museum, York; R. S. Carpenter, Hollywood, Birmingham; Richard M. Casserley, Berkhamsted; Andrew Choong, Curator, National Maritime Museum, Greenwich, London; Stephen Cole, Local Studies Department, Cardiff Central Library; Chris Collard, Rumney, Cardiff (former editor of *Ship Ahoy* magazine); Katrina Coopey, Local Studies Department, Cardiff Central Library; Callum Couper, Port Manager, Associated British Ports, Cardiff; Michael Crabb, Easton, Portland, Dorset; Viv Crabb, Pontypridd, Mid Glamorgan; John Curle, Wyke Regis, Dorset; Ted Darke, Easton, Portland, Dorset; John Davey, Managing Director, Stevedoring & Cargo Handling, Cardiff Docks; Martyn Farquhar, Portland, Dorset; Fleet Air Arm Museum, Yeovilton, Somerset; David Fletcher, Curator, Tank Museum, Bovington, Dorset; John Fry, Ely, Cardiff; J. and J. Collection, c/o D. K. Jones, Mountain Ash, Mid Glamorgan; Brian Gambles, Birmingham Central Library; Stuart Hadaway, Assistant Curator, Department of Research & Information, RAF Museum; Michael Hale, Woodsetton, Dudley; *Harbour Lights* magazine, Swansea; Cliff W. Harris, Porth, Mid Glamorgan; Frank Hornby, Sutton, Surrey; *Illustrated London News* Picture Library; Cliff C. James, Taffs Well, Mid Glamorgan; Mike Jarvis, Civil Engineer's Department, Associated British Ports, Cardiff; David Jenkins, Curator, National Waterfront Museum, Swansea; Derek K. Jones, Mountain Ash, Mid Glamorgan; Glyndwr G. Jones, Bromley, Kent; Mrs Jan Keohane, Archivist, Fleet Air Arm Museum, Yeovilton, Somerset; Lens of Sutton Association; Harold Lloyd, Sully, Vale of Glamorgan; Mrs Hillary Lloyd Fernandez (retired), Associated British Ports, Cardiff; Locomotive Club of Great Britain (Ken Nunn Collection); Doreen Luff, Cardiff; Tony Luff, Portland, Dorset; Keith Luxton, Taffs Well, Mid Glamorgan; David Mathew, Cardiff; Hywel Mathews, Pontypridd Library; Mrs L. Morris, Area Librarian, Pontypridd Library; National Railway Museum, York; Ordnance Survey Department, Southampton; John O'Brien, Pentwyn, Cardiff; Bill Osborn, Penarth, South Glamorgan; George Pearce, Grangetown, Cardiff; *Pontypridd and Llantrisant Observer*; Pontypridd Library, Mid Glamorgan; Alun G. Powell, Rhydyfelin, Pontypridd, Mid Glamorgan; Royal Air Force Museum, London; *The Railway Magazine*, London; Doug Richards, Pencoed, Mid Glamorgan; Keith Robbins, GWS, Didcot, Oxfordshire; Ken Shapley, Associated British Ports, Cardiff; *Ship Ahoy* magazine, Cardiff, South Glamorgan; Graham Stacey, LCGB, Egham, Surrey; Brian Stephenson, RAS Marketing, Ashford, Kent; Clive Thomas, Deputy Port Manager, Associated British Ports, Cardiff; R. E. Toop, Bath; Mrs Elaine Tuft, Trowbridge, Cardiff; John Wynn (retired), Wynn's (Heavy Haulage) Ltd, Newport, Gwent; Peter Wynn, Wynn's (Heavy Haulage) Ltd, Eccleshall, Staffordshire.

Associated British Ports, Cardiff, and its staff have always shown great hospitality to me during my many visits to them over the years, and recently two former members of staff have passed on. I would therefore like to offer my condolences to the widows of the late John B. Phelps and Norman Watts; both were true gentlemen, and it was an honour to have known them.

INDEX